Dedicated to my family
Christine, Brett, Matt, and Jacob

with special thanks to:
*Julie Chapman, Ed and Pat Miller,
Michael Schear, Bob Williamson,
Luke Cuccia, Pablo,
and Stackpole Books*

of Congress Cataloging-in-Publication Data

ob.
carving : an introduction / Bob Berry.
.   cm.
graphy: p.
0-8117-0839-X : $24.95
ood-carving—Technique. 2. Fishes in art. I. Title.
48   1988
dc19

88-12305
CIP

W9-CRQ-029

*LES,
GOOD LUCK
WITH YOUR FISH
CARVING !
BEST WISHES,*

Bob Berry

— Salt Water —

El Cajon, Ca.   — Bob Berry —
619- 588 7141
2261 Runabout Pl.
El Cajon, Ca.

FISH CARVING
an introduction

Bob Berry

Stackpole

P
St
Ca
P.C
Ha

All
por
incl
retri
All i
Kelke

Printe

10   9

Contents

1 Introducing the Artist 1

2 The Importance of Reference 6

3 Trophy Rainbow Trout   Following step-by-step
instructions for carving a beginner's project 10

4 Brown Trout   Creating a competition-type carving,
using detailed instructions 27

5 Brook Trout   Making a carving featuring
open-mouth detail 54

6 Bluegill   Carving a large-scaled fish 61

7 Largemouth Bass   Making a full decorative
competition-type scenario 74

8 Lionfish and Queen Angelfish   Doing a saltwater
reef fish composition 85

9 Gallery 109

10 Additional Patterns 125

11 Afterword 133

Bibliography 134

Appendices 136

A Note on the Patterns

All the fish patterns in this book are at 40 percent of life size. To make life-size carvings, you will need to enlarge the patterns by 250 percent (two and a half times). There are two ways to accomplish this. You can photocopy the pattern on a copying machine that enlarges, or you can buy a scaling device used by graphic designers to size photographs. An example is the Scaleograph, manufactured by the Brandt Corporation of New Orleans. It can be found in most art supply and graphic arts supply stores, and instructions are included.

All photographs by Bob Berry unless otherwise credited

Introducing the Artist

I became a fish carver by way of taxidermy. When I graduated from high school in 1964, I already had several years of amateur taxidermy experience, having taken the Northwestern School of Taxidermy mail order course at age twelve. Upon graduating from high school, I went to work for Lyons and O'Haver Taxidermy. They were—and still are—the leading marine taxidermists on the West Coast. I spent several years with them, working with birds, mammals, and fish. The influence of Hughie Lyons and Mike O'Haver was substantial. Besides demanding quality, they helped me train myself to be productive.

Back in the early sixties, we were doing fish skin mounts. We carved the bodies for most of our smaller fish out of balsa wood. Patterns were drawn directly from the fish on butcher paper, cut out, transferred to the balsa wood, and cut on the bandsaw. They were then rough-rounded by tilting the bandsaw table. As you'll see, this is basically how I carve my fish today. After the mounted fish were dried and detailed to fix imperfections, we painted them with automotive lacquers because all natural colors fade to a dark gray when a fish dies. I began my painting with a silver base-coat primer. All the natural colors and patterns were then painted on.

The photo in this chapter of a steelhead trout is a mount of a personal trophy I caught in the summer of 1965. I mounted it as soon as I returned from that fishing trip. Over twenty-three years later, it's still in pretty good condition. It shows many of the things I'm doing now with my

The steelhead trout is a mount of a personal trophy I caught in the summer of 1965.

fish carvings. It's the first fish I remember mounting with an S-curve in it. The body was carved out of balsa wood (similar to the brown trout in this book). It was scaled with silver paint and a small brush, highlighting each scale.

It was also about 1965 when I made my first duck decoy. Knowing absolutely nothing about decoy carv-

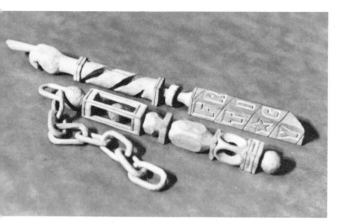

"Short Timer" sticks I made for Army buddies in Vietnam.

ing didn't stop me. I made a drake green-winged teal, and I still have it. If you have a good imagination you can recognize it as a green-winged teal. I made quite a few decoys for people at $20.00 to $25.00 apiece back then.

My years at Lyons and O'Haver Taxidermy were interrupted by two years in the Army. I served in Vietnam in 1969 with the 25th Infantry Division, receiving the Army Commendation Medal and two Bronze Stars for valor. While there, I found a little time to do some whittling with my pocket knife. I used pine wood from mortar and artillery ammo boxes. Most of my carvings were given away as "Short Timer" sticks to friends who were ending their tours of duty.

Back home in 1970, I returned to work at Lyons and O'Haver. Something new had come about: They were doing some reproduction work with fish. I quickly got myself up to date on reproductions. About 1973 I

opened up my own taxidermy studio and specialized in fish reproductions. During the next few years, my shop, Animal Arts Taxidermy, reproduced hundreds upon hundreds of fish. My experience with fish grew almost daily.

I did some fish carving back in 1975. I carved a miniature marlin and a miniature marlin head mount for annual trophies for the San Diego Marlin Club. Room-temperature vulcanizing (RTV) rubber molds were made, and the trophies were reproduced in a solid urethane. I carved some other fish a little later, but only as prey for a bald eagle carving and an osprey carving.

Painting twenty-nine head mount reproductions.

After a few years, I closed my taxidermy shop and went to work for Doug Miller and his Wildlife World Museum in Monument, Colorado. Doug Miller was a very perceptive

A full-bodied carving reproduction of a blue marlin I did when I had my taxidermy shop.

person and allowed all of his artists (John Scheeler, William Koelpin, Bill Schultz, Gerald Balciar, and others) to pursue their ideas and create without guidelines. I had a perfect "Renaissance" job. I was working on a salary and my job was to mount birds, reproduce fish, and carve decoys. I had the freedom to do whatever I felt like doing, so long as it was done correctly.

Doug Miller was a major influence in guidance and encouragement in my fish carvings. He was also *the* collector and supporter of wildfowl carving for many years. All realistic-style decorative and decoy carvers

owe him thanks.

At this time, I was still doing a little decoy carving as a hobby. In 1975 I entered my first decoy carved for a show and won a blue ribbon with it in the amateur division. (It won three blue ribbons in amateur divisions at three different shows that year.) My friend Jim Sprankle won amateur ribbons that year also. Other winners of note were William Schultz and John Scheeler, open division. All three of these men have been a tremendous influence on me and my carving. Jim is always very helpful and encouraging. He carves wonderfully accurate decoys. Schultz's and

Scheeler's work, part of Doug Miller's Wildlife World Museum collection, was my inspiration to better work. Each man had a distinctly different style. Bill Schultz's was clean and neat, anatomically correct, and neatly painted. John Scheeler's accuracy and interpretation showed a little more surface contours and roughness. His raptors especially showed a fierce penetrating animation.

While I was still working at the Wildlife World Museum, my wife surprised me with our first trip to Hawaii. She bought the tickets and made all the plans. Her intention was to get me to relax and forget about wildlife and my work, but her plan was only partially successful. I did relax, but I took along my fins, mask, snorkel, and my Minolta Weathermatic underwater camera. It was there in Hawaii that I had my eyes opened.

I had always liked fish, but in Hawaii I was totally taken by the colors and beauty of the reef fish I saw during my underwater expeditions. There were enormous artistic possibilities in these incredibly colored and shaped fish. My decoy hobby had taught me that there was a great demand for bird carvings. Why not carve fish? I didn't know of anyone who was doing that kind of work, so I decided to try it myself. About six months after that first Hawaiian vacation, I did my first fish carving.

My very first fish carving was a moorish idol and a female bird wrasse. I used natural coral and shells, and Plexiglas for the pectoral fins. Doug Miller was surprised and pleased at the first fish carvings I did for him (I wouldn't tell him what I was working on; I just showed him the finished work). They won blue ribbons in a taxidermy show and displayed well at his museum.

My first fish carvings contained real coral and shells, but Doug suggested I carve everything. I began carving all my corals and shells, making my works total wood sculptures in the manner of the decorative bird carvings. I adopted the rules of the Ward Foundation for their decorative world pieces. My compositions are handmade almost entirely of wood, except for glass eyes and metal for structural support. I also try to keep to a minimum putties, epoxies, plastics, and so on.

Now I make my living full-time from fish carving. Although I often teach classes in carving, I spend most of my time doing work for galleries all across the U.S. My freedom to do as I wanted for the Wildlife World Museum has carried over to how I approach my carving today. I still carve what I want and then offer it for sale. Commissions are accepted but most are governed only by species and approximate size. I reserve all other artistic considerations. This seems to work very well and not to stymie my interest or creativity.

Just as there are favorite subjects in wildfowl carving, such as mallards, wood ducks, and Canada geese, there are popular and regional favorite fish subjects as well. Obviously, common game fish—largemouth bass, rainbow trout, brown trout—are quite popular

My first decoy, a drake green-winged teal.

as carving subjects. These are a major portion of my sales and commissions. Regional favorites such as sea trout, grayling, and Caribbean tropicals are generally sold to or requested by customers from these regions.

I enjoy doing new fish and putting into action some of the ideas I think about. It's the creativity and challenge of something new, interesting, or difficult that keeps me at my workbench hour after hour. I enjoy what I'm doing and get totally involved in each carving. I like the freedom to do the many exotics, especially the saltwater reef fish. These fish as a group have completely captured me. Their patterns, colors, textures, and reef habitat offer a

lifetime of new and interesting challenges and subject matter. I may be the first sculptor to seriously consider these fish as subjects. I know I won't be the last. Now many wildlife artists are beginning to discover these great fishes.

I try to be first with ideas and implementation of those ideas. My fish carvings are truly originals. I could do the same fish over and over again but never would; all my carvings are one of a kind. I have no enthusiasm for doing identical pieces; besides, the combinations of fish, corals, and shells are unlimited, making it easy to create a totally different carving each time.

The Importance of Reference

The key to an accurate carving is reference. In order to carve something, you must know what it looks like. The consistent winners in bird carving competitions are the ones who really know their subjects.

Through the years, as a taxidermist and now a sculptor specializing in fish, I've made a concerted effort to build my own library and photo reference files.

Collecting reference materials is a never-ending process. I've got shelves full of books, but they can add up to quite an expense. Some books I've bought for a few good photos that are in them. I've got several very good reference identification books, but none show more than one or two photos of a particular fish I may want to carve. A single photo is not enough.

I've subscribed to a variety of outdoor magazines (for example, *Skin Diver* and *Ocean Realm,* and many hunting and fishing magazines) and over the years have accumulated hundreds and hundreds of photos that I've clipped and filed. Ninety-nine percent of these photos are of our common North American game fish. I'll still buy a copy of one of these magazines now and then for a good photo. When I'm clipping, I'll take any photo of something that may be of some

value to me, such as a photo of a dragonfly or a lily pad and flower. These photos come in very handy when it comes time to add a little something to set the scene.

The very best thing to do is go out and get your own reference materials. Go catch a fish, photograph it, make notes on colors and patterns, draw patterns from it, freeze and keep it, make a study cast of it, and so forth. Collect a few stones and maybe a shell or snail, a crayfish, plants, driftwood, sand. Once you have these things, you eliminate any guesswork in your carving composition. This active field collecting gives you an understanding of nature, which will show in your carvings.

I began taking underwater photos of fish and reef life on my first trip to Hawaii. I also began collecting shells and coral samples. The following year, I took along a small rod and reel and caught a few specimens. I also collected some with a Hawaiian sling (a type of spear). Every year I add to my reference materials. I do this any time I go somewhere, whether it's Baja California, the Florida Keys, or Alaska. This way, I develop references that I can trust. I also ensure accuracy of my compositions.

The idea of understanding nature

and knowing about other animals on the reef besides the fish is only obtained by diving on a reef. Most people dive or snorkel and look about the reef, pointing at fish and coral heads from a distance, not noticing the small cowrie in a crevice or the flatworm under a coral head. When I go diving in Hawaii, I'll stay in the water for hours. I look in holes, under rocks and coral. I get right into the reef as close as I can. When I collect, I take only a few specimens; one or two humpback cowries are enough.

In Kauai, Hawaii I found two beautiful samples of lace coral. One specimen, collected in Poipu Beach, a heavy surge and surf zone without a barrier reef, is very sturdy, with short, stunted branching. The other lace coral specimen was collected in calm waters in back of the barrier reef near Princeville, Kauai. It shows a dramatic difference from the coral collected in a surge and surf zone. The calm-water specimen is very delicate and shows a lot of branching. Knowing the difference between these kinds of coral helps to add accuracy to your carvings.

Other kinds of coral that are worth collecting are star corals, vase corals, and cauliflower corals. Star corals grow in large solid nonbranching coral heads and can form reefs fifty to one hundred feet across. They can grow fairly flat and lumpy or in pyramid-shaped mounds. They range in color from yellow to brown and green. Vase coral is aptly named, for it looks like a vase. Cauliflower coral has depth and spacing between the

Two examples of lace coral collected in Kauai, Hawaii. The one on the left was collected in calm waters; the one on the right, in a heavy surge and surf zone.

There are several species of star corals, and many look alike.

Vase coral (left rear) and finger coral (right rear). At left front is a star coral; at right front, finger coral with fingers fused together.

Three of my favorite sea stars to carve.

A sampling of my cowrie shells.

Cauliflower coral.

branches. As cauliflower coral grows, it will avoid contact with other branches, but it fills the voids with lobes that are the start of a new branch.

Sea fans are gorgonians or "soft corals." Unlike the stony corals mentioned above, they have a flexible skeletal structure that moves with the water currents. They are flat and grow at a 90-degree angle to the prevailing surge or current. They range in colors from pink to brown, with purple being very common.

Sea stars can enhance your carvings, but be sure you know the habitat of each one. Color reference photos of the live animal are also important, because the natural colors fade when the specimens are dried.

Cowrie shells are my favorites of all shells. Their natural smooth glassy surface makes them very attractive. This adds a great deal of interest to a heavily textured base. The shells are relatively easy to carve and not par-

This fan-shaped coral consists of branches fused together.

ticularly difficult to paint either. Some lend themselves to hand painting and some are better painted with an airbrush.

Other shells that can add to your displays are cone shells, spindle shells, tun shells, and black murex. The cone shells are simple to carve but tend to be fairly time-consuming to paint. The knobby spindle shell presents a shape for thoughtful control in carving and painting. A tun shell needs special care in carving to keep its spiral shape and ridges smooth and accurate. The black murex is a complicated carving piece but paints fairly easily. My shells are chosen for carving by size, shape, color, texture, ease of carving and painting, and accuracy. Some shells, like some corals and some fish, are not practical to carve.

My descriptions of the various corals and shells are not intended to be scientific. I have books that identify the various species, describe them, and give other information. These facts are helpful, but the most important thing is to know where and how these animals live. It's necessary to understand nature to be able to portray it successfully. Besides, field studies are a lot of fun.

The sea fan.

Sea horse composition.

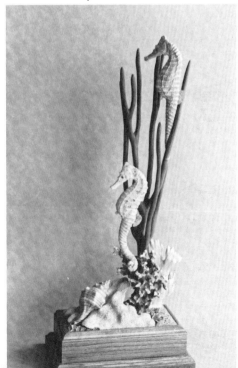

3

Trophy Rainbow Trout

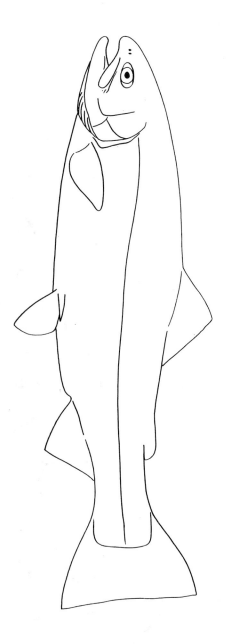

About the Pattern: My objective with this carving was to carve a one-sided trophy fish. The first step was to catch a trophy fish. This one happened to be my four-year-old son's first trout. (Brett caught three fish that day, while I was skunked.)

Once I had a fish, I drew my pattern directly from it. An accurate pattern is the first important step to an accurate carving. The pattern was developed by plotting countless measurements from fish to paper. I gave special attention to proper proportion and shape. I counted and drew in the individual fin rays, and copied the spot pattern accurately.

Carving: Since this is the first of several carving projects in this book, it is intended to be the simplest. Also, since I expect that my son will be carrying this carving to school year after year for show and tell, it has to be durable. I've decided on one-piece construction with fairly thick fins.

1. This photo shows my paper pattern cut out and the profile drawn on two-inch jelutong wood. Two-inch is plenty thick since I intend to keep the fish in a fairly flat pose.

2. Using a bandsaw, I cut out the side view. I've found that a ¼-inch skip tooth blade works best for me.

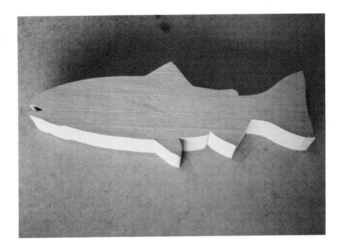

3. Considering the wood and the action I want, I sketch in a centerline of the fish, not a centerline of the wood. Notice the long clean-flowing S-curve. The head will be slightly out and the tail curved back in.

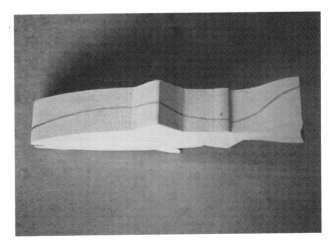

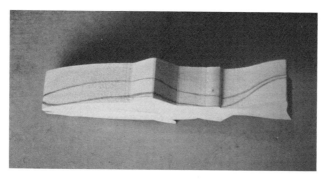

4. With the centerline established, I sketch in the front half of the body, top view. If your centerline is too close to the front to allow for full dimensions, adjust it back after sketching in the front half top view.

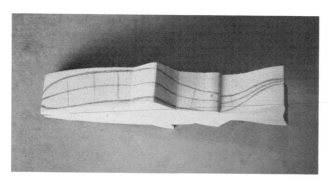

5. Now sketch in the back half top view. This can be "eyeballed" or it can be plotted by using a series of points on the front half and plotting them the same measurement across the centerline on the back half. Keep in mind that these points will occur on a square or 90-degree radius from the centerline. The pectoral and pelvic fins should be plotted onto the wood and allowed for in the top view.

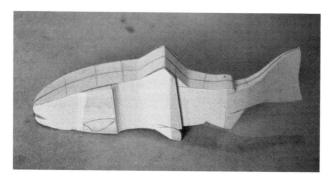

6. Starting at the head, I cut the top view. Notice that the pectoral and pelvic fins extend beyond the fish's body.

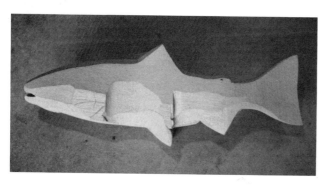

7. By tilting the table on the bandsaw, I can save myself some time by removing some wood. Remember that it's easy to cut off a fin if you're not careful. Some parts of the body you will not be able to rough cut because of the fins being part of the one-piece carving.

8. Using a Foredom tool, I begin to rough out the fish's body, starting by removing the wood I had to leave on the body during the bandsawing. I work to establish the pectoral and pelvic fins and continue the body shape. I like the large ¾-inch carbide cylinder for this step.

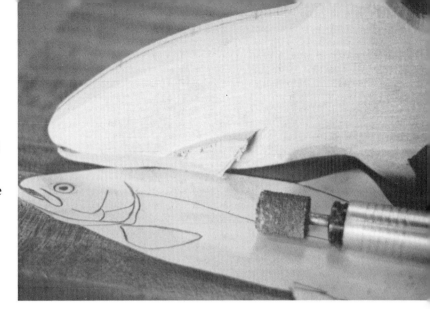

9. The wood is removed to conform to the top view.

10. Using a ⅝-inch carbide ball, I cut to within ⅛ inch of the centerline on the centerline fins.

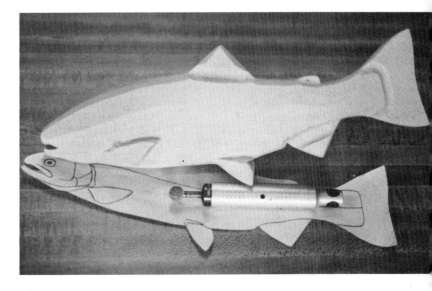

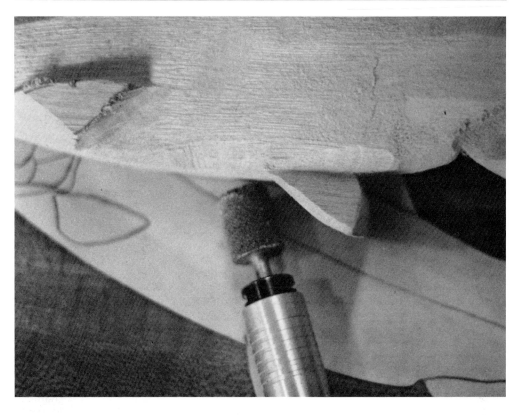

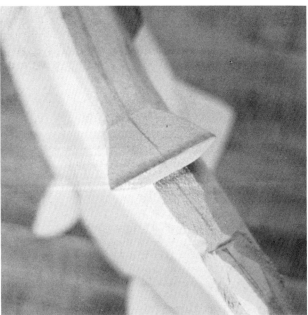

11. Now I turn my attention to the pelvic fins. I use a ¾-inch carbide cylinder to establish the top side of both fins. This is a little tricky. You must make the tip of the fin the widest point.

12. This photo shows the pelvic fins from the bottom after this operation.

13. Using the same cutter, I cut out the underside in between these fins. The pelvic girdle is V-shaped at the base of the fins. I cut it out, leaving the fins approximately ¼ inch thick.

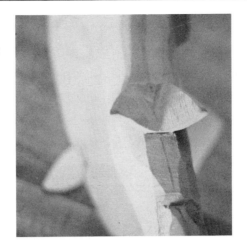

14. This photo shows the pelvic fins from the side front. Notice how the fins flare out.

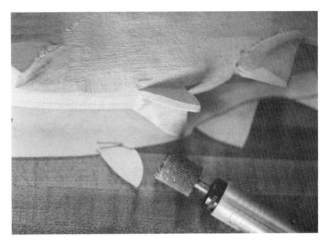

15. I cut around the pectoral fin, being careful not to cut into the actual body.

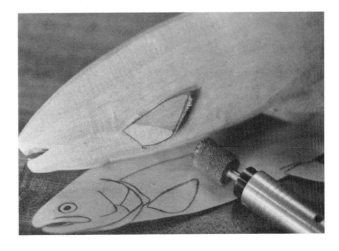

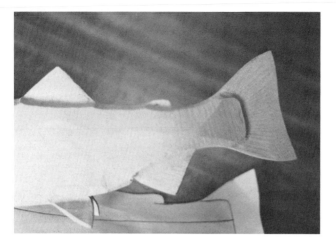

16. I now thin down all the centerline fins to about ¼ inch, using a ⅝-inch carbide ball. I work in the direction of the fin rays. This helps me see and feel the fish hidden in the wood.

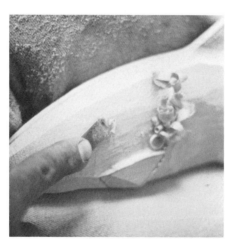

17. With all the fins established, I switch to knives and chisels to shape the body. This can be done with a variety of tools (Foredom, rasp, sanding disk, and so on), but I think I maintain the long smooth body contours better with my hand tools. I can feel areas that need to be shaped.

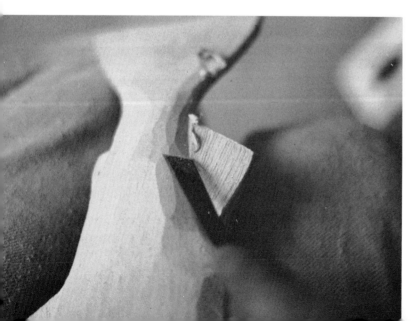

18. This photo shows how I can establish the clean sharp lines where the fins touch the body. This is not the fin base. It is the back bottom edge of the anal, dorsal, adipose, and pelvic fins. For purposes of strength, I like to have these fins lying against the body. It is quite normal for the fish to have its fins touch the body in this manner.

19. As I continue rounding the body, I'm careful not to carve across the centerline anywhere. Carving across the centerline would change the side profile that was carefully drawn and cut on the bandsaw.

20. This photo shows the body contours beginning to take shape. As I work with my hands over the entire fish, I'm able to find edges and bumps or dips that I blend together or work to remove.

21. Now that I've got my basic fish shape (or blank), I can turn to individual details. I transfer the head structure lines to the wood. Keep in mind that these have to be adjusted to account for the roundness of the fish's shape. For a one-sided fish, it's not necessary to carve any details into the back side. It will be finished around the belly and over the back, but fin and head details will not be put in. I would suggest this plan if this is your first fish carving. This will give you the satisfaction of completing the project, and you won't have to concentrate on carving the opposite side to a perfect symmetrical match.

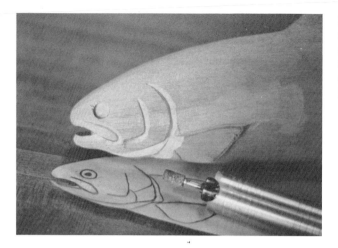

22. I use a ⁵⁄₁₆-inch carbide cylinder to cut in the relief of the head structure. I cut the eye socket, maxillary and opercular bones, and the branchiostegals.

23. I use my knife and chisel to blend these cuts back into the fish.

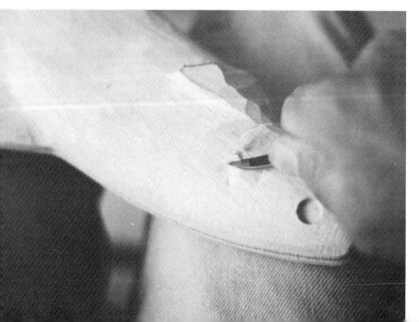

24. After working these areas back into the fish, I thin down the operculars.

25. Using a ⁷⁄₁₆-inch carbide ball, I shape the fins. I try to give them as much curve and shape as I can.

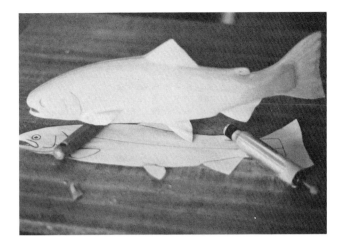

26. The trailing edge of the tail showing the wavy shape and thinned edge.

27. At this point, I sand the entire fish. I use 60-grit paper, and sand and blend the entire fish, being careful around the head and fins. It's best to sand with long strokes at several different angles.

28. Now, with the fish in a reasonably accurate shape, I can proceed to detail it to any extent I wish. This project will have a minimum of texture and time-consuming details. The body will be a smooth-sanded finish. I'll put in desired details with paint. Using a carbide disk, I cut in some fin rays.

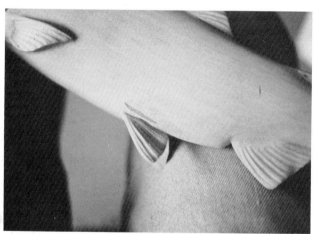

29. Notice how the fin rays are curved. Always try to avoid straight lines.

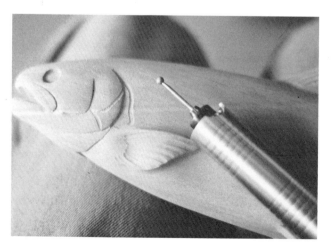

30. I define the individual opercular bones and the shoulder girdle with a small ruby ball. Notice I've penciled in the branchiostegal rays.

31. I cut the branchiostegal rays in with a diamond cylinder. The mouth is hollowed out with a larger ruby ball.

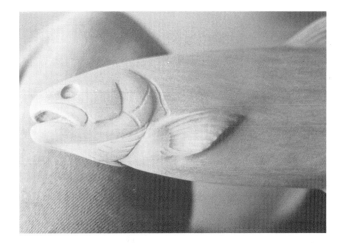

32. I set the eye in a bed of oil clay. It gives me unlimited time to get a proper set. I use Tohickon FE 135 fish eyes, as they are the best you can get. (See Appendix for address.) To set the eye, tip it in slightly at the bottom and front and point the pupil off the end of the snout. Fill around the eye with a plastic wood filler and allow it to dry before trimming and sanding. Be careful not to scratch the eye with sandpaper.

33. This photo shows the finished fish, sealed with a clear lacquer sanding sealer. I usually give it a coat, let it dry, then lightly sand and defuzz and give it a second coat. The fish is now ready to paint.

Painting: I chose to paint this fish by hand with acrylics. I prefer Liquitex paints and use mostly Grumbacher white bristle oil brushes, flats and rounds.

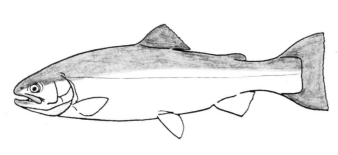

34. Start with Neutral Gray value 4.0. Paint the back of the fish. Since this is a background base color, I use it straight from the tube with just enough water to wet the bristles. Stop the paint at a line through the eye extending the length of the body about one-third down from the top. Paint the dorsal, adipose, and caudal fins. Splash a little paint around the mouth area.

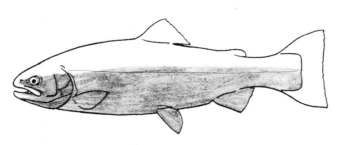

35. The second color is Neutral Gray value 8.0. Paint the rest of the fish with the pale gray. Be sure to run both colors around the back side.

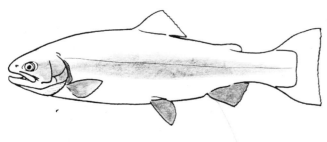

36. I use Light Magenta value 7.0 to paint in the pink rainbow stripe on the side. Paint the lower fins also. Try to have blended edges on your pink stripe.

37. The fourth color is Prism Violet value 3.0. Paint very sparingly. Make it a little blotchy on the operculars. Add a very thinned-down stripe down the center of the pink stripe.

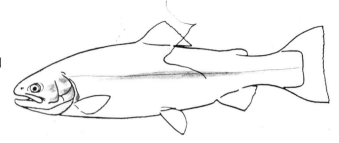

38. Color number five is Vivid Red Orange value 6.0. Paint it over the pink rainbow stripe using a thinned-down wash. Pick up a little more paint in the brush and darken the color on the operculars. Paint the lower fins with a wash, then add a little more color to the bases of those fins. Try to blend to the edges. Don't cover the pink entirely.

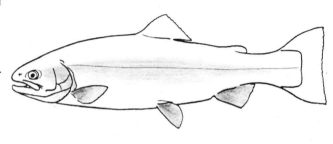

39. The sixth color is Iridescent White. Paint it over all light-colored areas. Two or three thin washes are better than one heavy coat.

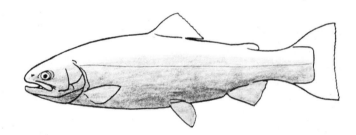

40. The next color is a mixture of Chromium Oxide Green, Iridescent Gold, and Neutral Gray value 4.0. Combine these in about equal parts and paint the darker upper one-third of the fish.

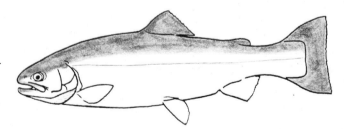

23

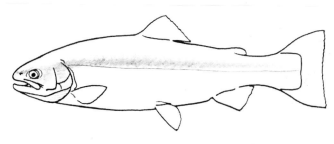

41. Now, using Iridescent Gold, paint using a dry brush technique over the line where the green back meets the pink stripe. (Dry brushing is best described as no water and very little paint applied in almost a scrubbing motion.) Paint a few wispy strokes over the opercular area as well.

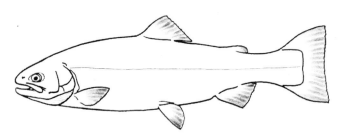

42. Using a very dry brush with Neutral Gray value 8.0, brush across the trailing edge of all the fins. This should blend out halfway to the base.

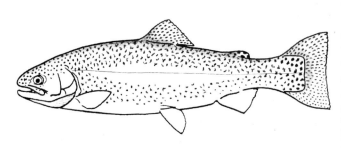

43. I use a No. 1 round synthetic bristle brush to paint the spotting. The spotting changes size and shape from head to tail. Using Ivory Black, try to copy the spotting reasonably accurately for size, shape, and number. Once the spotting is on, dry brush and darken the very top of the back and the base of the dorsal and caudal fins.

44. Using a felt-tipped silver-paint marking pen, I put in a scale pattern over the body from the back down to where the black spots end. Develop the scales in a lazy "S" diagonal line. Once you start, continue straight through until you finish. If you have a black spot or two that are not just right, you can correct them with this silver scaling. This pen paint dries a little slowly, so be careful how you handle your fish while scaling. You may be able to find these pens at your local stationery store. Wildlife Artist Supply Company carries silver and gold paint marking pens (see Appendix).

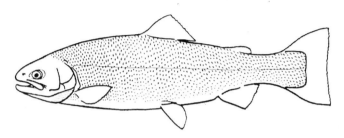

45. If your fish seems too bright, go back over the upper back with Black using a dry brush. Do a light dry brushing of Pink on the side and put Iridescent White very faintly on the transition area where the silver scaling blends into the belly. This should tone down the silver scaling and bring back a little color where needed.

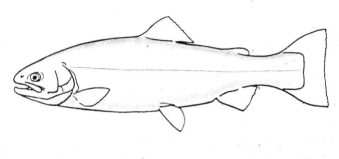

46. Using Titanium White, I paint the white fleshy membrane areas around the mouth, eye, and operculum. I also paint the valleys between the branchiostegal rays. Dry brush the very tips of the pectoral, pelvic, and anal fins. Using a stippling technique, I paint the bottom belly area.

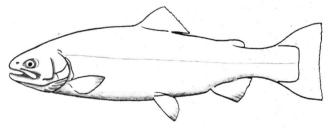

47. I clean the eye with a knife and finish with a couple coats of gloss lacquer. The finished fish is mounted on a piece of driftwood and hung on a wall in my son's room.

Finishing: The trout is now finished. The overall presentation is similar to a taxidermy mount. I've tried to put the fish in a relaxed swimming pose, and painted it to make it look as natural as possible. The soft S-curve of the body, the minimal up-down action typical of taxidermy, and the handling of the fins make this a very visually pleasing carving.

4

Brown Trout

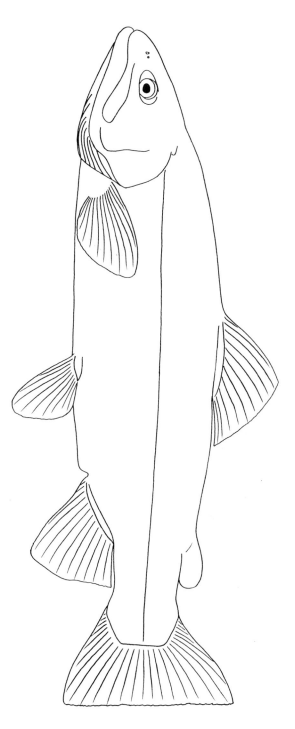

About the Pattern: This particular
brown trout is one of my favorite patterns. The pattern was drawn from a
specimen given to me by Jim Hall,
famous taxidermist from Idaho Falls,
Idaho. It's almost identical to a fish I
caught from the East Walker River
when I was a kid. I mounted that trout
many years ago using a dry-sand-fill
method. It looked very much like a
sweet potato with fins. To me, this pattern's like a personal trophy, and a
reminder of many hours spent along
Eastern Sierra trout streams.

Carving: I cut a paper pattern from
this seventeen-and-a-half inch trophy
brown trout. I'll be inserting the fins.
The body will be cut from jelutong
and the fins from bandsaw scraps. In
addition to the power tools and hand
tools, I'll be using a burning tool to
achieve more details.

1. This photo shows my paper pattern for my seventeen-and-a-half-inch trophy brown trout.

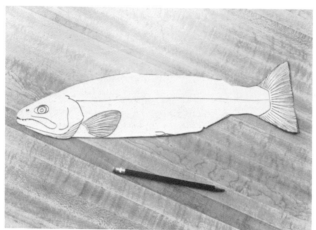

2. Before tracing onto the wood, I fold all the fins back, since all the fins will be inserted.

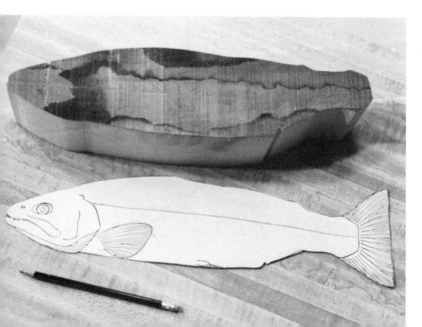

3. Side profile cut from three-inch jelutong. Notice that even the tail will be inserted.

4. Top view sketched in. I draw in the centerline first to get the desired body curvature. Then I draw in the sides equidistant from the centerline. The head area should be straight. The body curves should be long and flowing. I prefer a slight S-curve.

5. Top view bandsawed out.

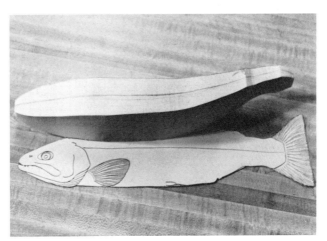

6. This photo shows the square-cut blank. Notice the body curvature and clean smooth cuts.

7. I tip the bandsaw table about 20 degrees and remove thin slices to begin shaping the body. I stay at least ¼ inch from the centerline. This will leave at least a ½-inch plane around the body on the centerline. If you cut closer, your fish will have a pointed back or belly or both.

8. This photo shows a head-on view after the 20-degree-angle cut around the centerline. Notice how the angled planes begin to establish the back and belly. The bellies of trouts seem to be slightly flattened, so allow a wider margin on the belly cuts.

9. The second cut goes completely around at a 45-degree angle. I split the first plane in the middle of its flat surface.

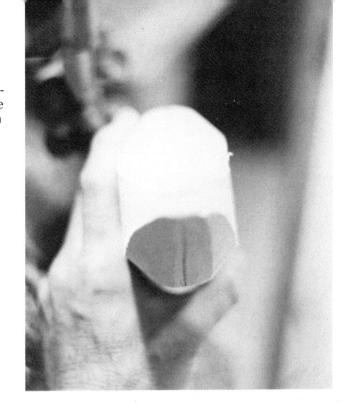

10. The third cut is a hand-held angle of about 75 degrees. Cut completely around the fish, splitting the flat surface of the second cut. This rough-rounds my fish quite quickly and reasonably accurately. Be careful while doing this, as bandsaws do not give fingers back.

11. This photo shows the three angled cuts. The centerline remains in a ½-inch-wide plane. Numbers 1, 2, and 3 show the 20-degree, 45-degree, and 75-degree angled cuts, respectively.

12. This photo shows the entire body rough-rounded on the bandsaw.

13. Using a ½-inch flat chisel, I round off all the edges of the bandsawed planes. I prefer the clean cutting and control of a chisel. As I work, I can feel areas that need to be rounded off. I have confidence in my skill with a Foredom but I do not like to use it at this stage. I think I get a truer shape by hand.

14. This photo shows the edges chiseled between the planes. It is obvious, by feel and by sight, that all the edges have been worked.

15. The centerline fins are drawn on thick-sliced stock. I use ⅜-inch- to ⅝-inch-thick wood. This allows for fin curve and shape. I try to have the wood grain run in the direction of the fin rays.

16. This photo shows the fins cut out. The arrows indicate the direction of the grain for strength. Notice the ¼-inch margin that will be inserted into the fish's body.

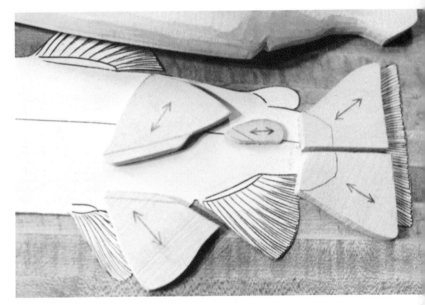

17. I cut the slots for the fins with a carbide saw/disk.

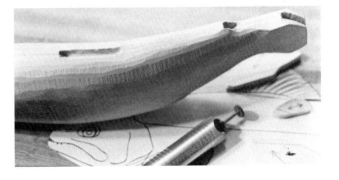

18. The fin bases are thinned down with a knife or chisel to fit snugly into the slots. You may have to match the curve of your fish to get a proper fit.

19. Install the fins with Bondo auto-body filler.

20. Using the paper pattern, trace on the structural details of the head. Do both sides, being sure to keep things even and symmetrical.

21. Using a ¼-inch carbide cylinder, I cut in these lines angled out to the rear. I cut about ⅛ inch deep.

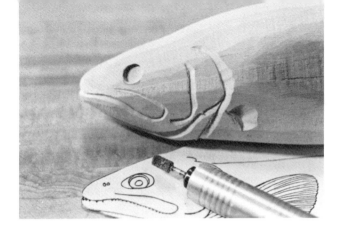

22. With a knife and chisel, I blend these square cuts back into the fish. Notice how the base for the pectoral fin is cut away. If you don't cut away this area, the pectoral fin will always look "stuck on." This is a very common error in fish carving.

23. This photo shows the wavy centerline established at the trailing edge of the tail. The thickness of the fins is essential to obtaining fin curvature or movement. Notice how I've utilized the entire thickness.

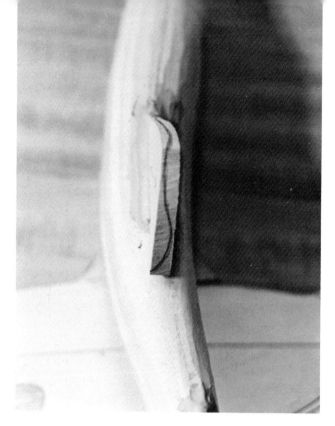

24. The dorsal fin from the top showing the centerline for carving and shaping. I make it a habit to draw these lines on. It keeps me from having fins that lack shape and form.

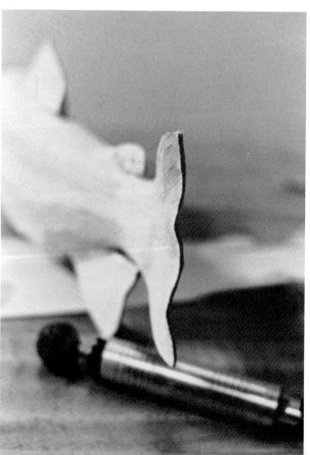

25. This photo shows the tail thinned and rough-shaped with a large carbide ball. Leave enough wood for further carving.

26. Side shot of the same process. Once the edges are defined, you simply remove the wood thickness from the fin base to the edges in a natural taper. The shadows from side lighting show the compound curves.

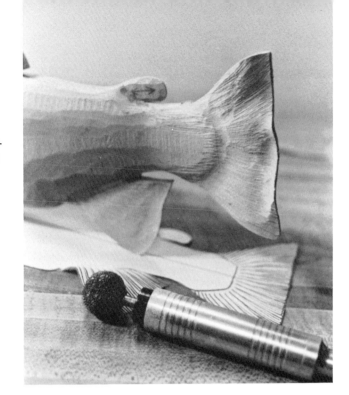

27. Using the same large carbide ball, hollow out the visceral and caudal dips. This is done with the large-diameter ball, as they are to be blended out quite wide. The end result should show subtle detail.

28. Taper and blend the edges of these dips out into the body.

29. At this point I sand and blend the entire body with 60-grit paper by hand. I prefer hand-sanding with long sanding strokes at a variety of angles. This allows me to achieve long soft curves. I avoid sanding drums and disks. The mechanical sanding devices do not give me the feel aspect that hand sanding does.

30. With a ruby ball or oval, dish out the eye trough. Establish the pectoral bone structure above the pectoral fin base and behind the operculum. Drop the opercular bone edges. Check with your reference for these details. I use frozen fish, photos, study casts, and my artistic license with a portion of experience.

31. Switch to a diamond cylinder and cut in the branchiostegal rays. You may wish to clean up and redefine some of the mouth and opercular areas.

32. With my burning tool on high, I burn in more details around the mouth and opercular areas. Be careful not to overdo it.

33. This photo shows the throat and branchiostegal rays.

34. At this point, I use fine sandpaper or sanding screen and sand the entire fish, except the fins. This should be the final sanding to soften all edges around the head and prepare the body for scale texturing.

35. Now I turn my attention back to the fins. I give them an accurate tapered thinness. I use a ½-inch carbide ball and work in the direction of the fin rays.

36. Notice how the use of the ½-inch ball gave me a couple smaller ripples in the upper half of the tail.

37. Once the fins are shaped, I cut in the fin rays with a carbide disk. I try to carve in the proper number of fin rays. (The first two or three are quite short and fleshy and not really discernible.) I try to create an arc or curve in each individual ray.

38. Using a disk-shaped stone, slightly rounded at the edge, I begin splitting each ray with two or three strokes. Notice the anal fin in this photo. The splitting should run down the ridges about two-thirds of the way from the edge to the base.

39. Changing to a sharp-edged stone, I cut and split the rays on the outer one-third of the fins. The sharper stone will cut a deeper V-shape and break through the trailing edges, giving a very natural look to the fins.

40. Illustration of "whole, two-thirds, one-third" rule. The use of three cutters, one over another, creates different physical and visual details from the base of the fin out to the edge.

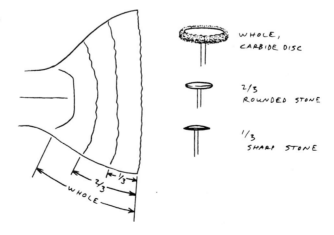

WHOLE, CARBIDE DISC

2/3 ROUNDED STONE

1/3 SHARP STONE

WHOLE

2/3

1/3

41. I sketch in the lateral line and establish it by cutting with a drum-shaped stone on either side. This makes a thin raised vein along the length of the fish. Do not cut or burn in a groove. The lateral line is always raised. Sand and blend out the edges into the sides if necessary.

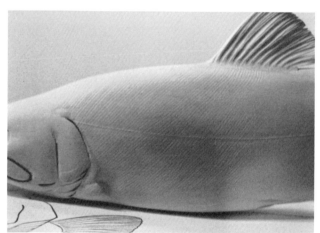

42. To carve in scales, I use a small stone ball. I cut a series of diagonal parallel lines in one direction over the entire side. This photo shows the lines cut in back to the dorsal fin.

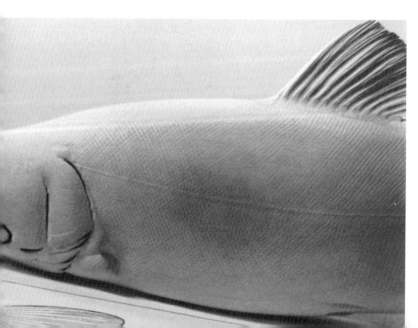

43. This photo shows the second set of diagonal scale lines being cut in over the first. This leaves a diamond-shaped grid over the fish. It's quite effective on a fine-scaled fish such as a trout. (If you're heavy-handed, lightly sand with a worn piece of sanding screen.) Cutting in the scales on a trout is time-consuming and tedious, very much like burning in feathers on a bird. You must work slowly and carefully and be consistent throughout the entire process.

44. At this point, I set the fish aside and set up a base for it. I choose a piece of driftwood with character that will complement my fish but not overwhelm it or distract from it. The driftwood is cut flat on the bottom. Then a free-form particle-board base is cut. Rocks are cut from the pile of odd-shaped scrap that accumulates around my bandsaw. I shape and texture them as I go along. I use my sampling of real rocks as models for shapes and textures.

45. The rocks are glued down with carpenter's glue. The driftwood is secured with screws and remains removable. With the rocks glued into place, I cut around and between them with the bandsaw.

46. With a mallet and a chisel, I shape the bottom part of the rocks. The idea is to remove all the vertical bandsaw cuts and create depth around the edge of the base.

47. This photo shows the variety of sizes, shapes, and textures in my rocks.

48. I cover the seams with Bondo and then shape and texture each individual rock.

49. With the base carved, I cut out my fin pairs: pectorals and pelvics. Thicker stock allows for more curvature in the fins. These measured just over ⅜-inch thick.

50. Using penciled guide-lines, I chip-carve a shape into one side of all four fins.

51. The fin in the foreground has been chip-carved on its reverse side. Notice its curvature.

52. Using a ⅝-inch carbide ball, I thin and shape the fins. From this point, I use the same procedures as on all the other centerline fins.

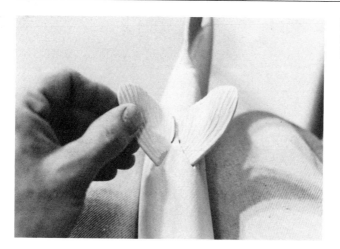

53. Just as with the centerline fins, I cut slots and fit the fins into them.

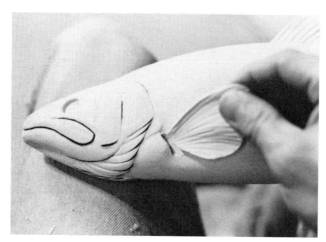

54. Pectoral fin is fit into slot cut into the body.

55. I install the fins with Bondo. I usually set all four fins at once, as the fit is fairly snug. If you're not fast enough or you mix your Bondo too hot, you may have to do the fins in pairs or individually.

56. While waiting for my fins to set up, I noticed how thin the tail was in a couple of spots. These thin spots will get a soaking of Superglue. Notice the uneven edge of the tail.

57. I use Tohickon FE 135 fish eyes in almost all my fish. I keep plenty in stock. Some are clear flint that I can paint myself for special fish or color variations. Tohickon Glass Eyes will also paint custom eyes upon request.

58. I locate the nostrils on one side and then plot them on the other side by drawing lines perpendicular to the centerline across the head, and then on a line of the proper level from the eye to the end of the snout.

59. I use ¼-inch threaded rod to support most of my fish. It gives both plenty of strength and a minimal point of attachment. I usually secure it in the base or the driftwood and drill a ¼-inch hole in the fish. Ninety percent of the time, the rod must be bent with pliers or channel locks before installing.

60. This photo shows the completed fish and base. The carving is ready to be painted after sealing with a clear sanding sealer. Polytranspar™ W5400 Clear Wood Sealer works quite well. Wildlife Artist Supply Company carries this; see Appendix.

61. Top view of carving. Notice the random rock placement and free-form base, the rod connection, and so on.

62. Front view.

63. Top front view.

64. Back side view. The natural branch will be removed when the rocks are painted. It will then be permanently attached, filled in and detailed at its seam, and painted to blend.

65. Tail view. Notice the curves in the fins, and the variety of size and texture in the rocks.

66. Head detail. Notice the nostrils, filled and shaped around the eye.

Painting: The brown trout is painted the way I remember that trophy fish I caught many years ago. I've got a couple good photos of stream fish showing these deep intense colors and patterns.

The base rocks are painted with Neutral Gray value 5.0, Ivory Black, Raw Umber, Burnt Umber, Raw Sienna, Titanium White, and modeling paste. I use the modeling paste with color to fill and further texture the rocks. I work in a variety of ways—wet on wet, dry brush, washes, stippling, single colors, multiple colors—trying anything to get an effect. The driftwood is also painted to blend with the entire setting. The light grays as they appear naturally are dry colors. I try to get a wet underwater mossy color to the wood by using washes of Chromium Oxide Green, Raw Umber, and a Neutral Gray.

After sealing the carved fish with a clear lacquer sanding sealer, I begin the painting with two coats of Neutral Gray value 5.0. Usually, the first coat doesn't cover completely. The second coat is more of a wash than the first coat.

67. Using Raw Umber, I darken the back and all the fins. I make the color darker at the fin bases, then blend to the edges. After blowing it dry with a hair dryer, I give the entire fish a medium wash.

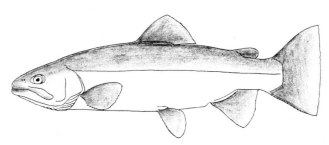

68. I mix Chromium Oxide Green, Raw Umber, and Iridescent Gold and paint the back. This blends out at a line about one-third down through the eye. I rinse my brush and drag some color out on the dorsal and caudal fins.

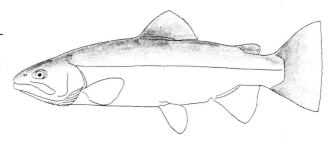

69. Bronze Yellow is the next color. I paint the belly and the outer edges of the lower fins and the tail. This should blend out in a dry brushing at mid-side.

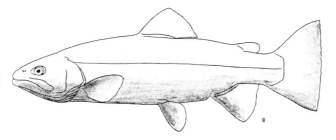

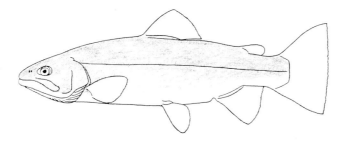

70. I dry brush Iridescent Gold over the back and side, but not on the belly or the fins.

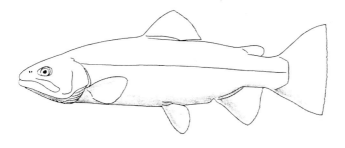

71. Yellow Orange is next. Dry brush the belly, the lower fins, and the bottom of the tail. Keep this close to the leading edges of the lower fins.

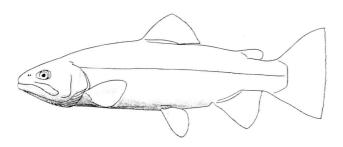

72. Using Turner's Yellow, dry brush the lower jaw and front belly, blending into the Yellow Orange. This should establish the background colors.

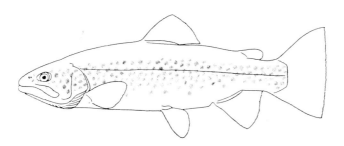

73. Using Iridescent Silver, I stipple in the silver halos that surround the black and red spotting. I use a No. 3 round white-bristle oil-painting brush for this. Check with your reference photos for accuracy and patterns.

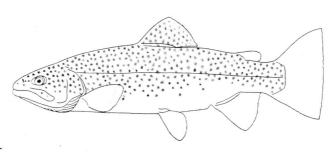

74. With a small round soft-bristle brush, paint in the spotting with Ivory Black. Try to get a variety of spot shapes. The spots vary on individual specimens. In general, they run right on up out of the silver halos and cover the back. They are usually smaller and less frequent from the head back to the dorsal fin. The dorsal fin is usually spotted as well.

75. Red Oxide is next. Paint in the red spots on the side, adipose fin, and upper tail edge. The red spots can be very bright, nearly black, or not present at all. They're usually confined to the side where the halos are, and on the tail and adipose fin. Avoid putting in too many red spots.

Finishing: I use a gold paint marking pen with a fine tip to scale the fish. Scale the back and side down to and around the lowest spots. This will create an interesting and accurate edge where the yellows from the belly meet the gold scaling. Work slowly, developing a rhythm and pattern. Don't stop until you've completed an entire side. Shake your pen occasionally.

When the gold scaling is dry, use a Raw Umber wash over the back and side, heaviest on center back. Avoid creating an edge of umber on the yellows. The wash should not go into the yellows.

Now go back and repaint the silver halos with a small round brush. Then repaint the black and red spotting. Paint white in the mouth membrane areas and around the operculars. I dry brush and stipple the belly just in back of the branchiostegals and the fleshy throat area with white. The fin edges are lightened very slightly as well. A little dry brush "doodling" around the eye and operculars with silver and gold iridescents defines some of these areas.

The finished fish is given two coats of high gloss lacquer, allowed to dry, and then permanently installed on the base. A hardwood base, cut, routed, and finished, is then added to complete the entire carving.

5

Brook Trout

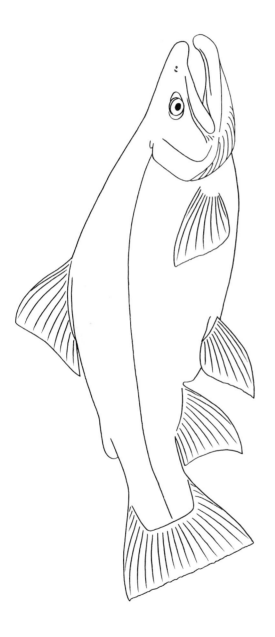

About the Pattern: The pattern for my brook trout was drawn from a specimen I collected in Colorado. It's the biggest brookie I've ever caught. It came from a small stream choked with beaver dams high in the mountains. The brookie's bright colors remind me of the beautiful autumn colors of the aspens when I caught it.

Carving: The brook trout carving done for this chapter is an unfinished carving, showing all the steps I go through. It shows the fish from the bandsawed stages, fin bases, fin thinning, fin inserts, fin texturing, caudal and visceral dips, head structure, open mouth, scale texturing, and, finally, painting. I'll detach and re-attach the open mouth to achieve better detail there. I also show the elements of the base in various stages of development.

1. This photo shows the carving after several preliminary steps—drawing from pattern, bandsaw cutting, and shaping—have been completed.

2. This photo shows head detail. With an open mouth, I want to carve in something more than a simple hollowed-out cavity.

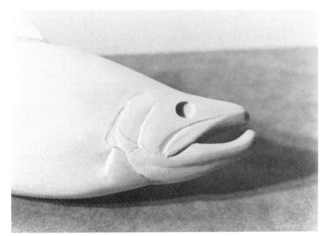

3. I cut the top of the head off at the corners of the mouth. It's far easier to carve the tongue, gill rakers, throat and vomerine teeth groups this way.

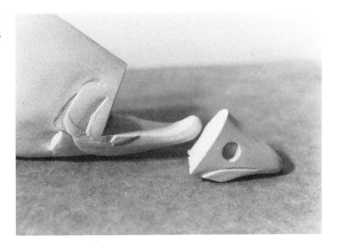

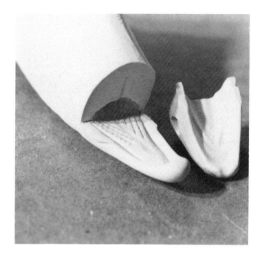
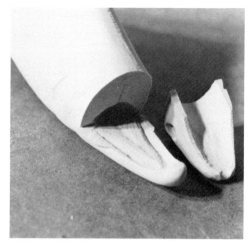

4. This photo shows the initial roughing out of the bottom and top of the mouth.

5. I carve in the appropriate details with ruby and diamond cutters.

6. The head is reattached with Bondo. Notice the seam. Just before reattaching, I carve away a little on each side of the bandsaw cuts, angled in. After attaching and filling, I make the seam wide. It will be invisible to the eye when detailed and painted. A thin straight-line seam would be visible through the paint.

7. Closeup of finished head.

8. The finished brook trout carving, front side.

9. The reverse side showing the basic steps in carving.

10. The finished carving with the front side painted. The base of the branch and a portion of the rock have been painted.

Painting: Painting a brook trout can be a little confusing for beginners. All the blended colors and patterns must be worked out and applied in a logical manner.

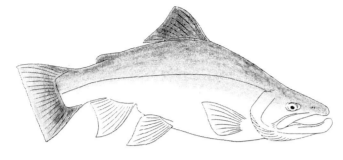

11. To begin with, I paint a two-tone Neutral Gray base coat. Use Neutral Gray value 4.0 for the back and value 7.0 for the belly. Blend them well on the side.

12. Paint the back with a combination of Chromium Oxide Green, Iridescent Gold, and Neutral Gray value 4.0. Blend this out at about the lateral line. Paint this over the dorsal and adipose fin also.

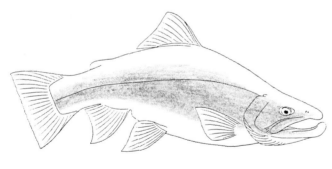

13. Using about a 50–50 mix of Yellow Oxide and Iridescent Gold, paint the side blended into the green/gold of the back. This should end at about the pectoral fin.

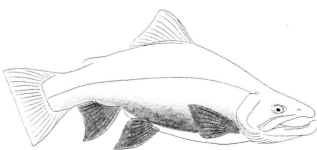

14. Using Red Oxide, paint the lower fins. Paint a wide blended line from the pectoral fin to the caudal peduncle. This should fade into the side.

15. Now, using Naphthol Crimson, deepen the Red Oxide at the leading edges of the fins and their bases, and on the red side-belly band at its bottom edge.

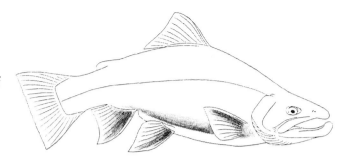

16. Paint the tail with Raw Sienna, then deepen the color of its base and edges with Red Oxide. Use Raw Sienna to lighten the edges of the other fins. Lighten the edge of the tail with a dry brushing of Yellow Oxide.

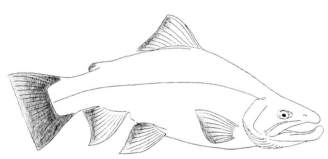

17. Using Titanium White, paint the belly. This is confined to an area from the vent to the branchiostegals, about the width of the pelvic fins. Paint in and around the mouth also.

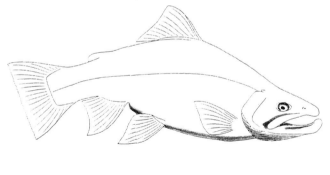

18. Using Ivory Black, dry brush the center back, dorsal fin, and base of tail. Paint the black stripe that separates the red and white along the belly. The edge with the white is slightly mottled and uneven but not blended. A stippling edge is best. The black tends to fade into the red but not necessarily blend with red or have a reddish tint. Paint the edge of the lower fins also. Leave enough space for the white markings. Paint the areas around the head as indicated by your references.

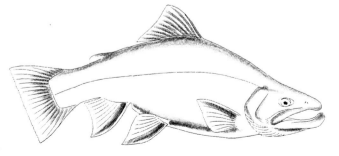

59

Finishing: The background colors are now all on. Repaint and touch up as needed. The vermiculations on the back are painted with Chromium Oxide Green and Turner's Yellow with a little gesso to make your color opaque. These markings will make or break your paint job. They twist and turn, and are about as wide as the spaces between them.

The yellow spotting on the side is done with Turner's Yellow and a little gesso again. A brook trout has red spots on its side (like a brown trout), but they are in the middle of blue spots. Use Light Blue Violet for the blue spot and Naphthol Crimson for the red spot in the center. Use Titanium White or gesso or both for the leading edges of the lower fins. The line between the white and black is sharp and crisp, but broken or "toothed" on close inspection. Paint white where needed around the mouth membrane areas. I paint in the teeth on all but my largest fish carvings. The tail has a tigerlike black pattern on the upper and lower edges that fades out as it goes in. Brook trout in their bright fall colors do not seem to have iridescent or metallic scaling.

6

Bluegill

About the Pattern: The pattern for the bluegill carving in this book is one drawn from a large specimen sent to me by Jim Hall. Bluegill make a very impressive carving. Their compact and compressed size makes them ideal carving subjects. Add in the details of the large scales and people are really attracted to them, probably as much by nostalgia as anything. Most fishermen undoubtedly caught stringers full of them in their youth.

Carving: Sometimes, getting started is the hardest part for me. If I don't have a preconceived plan, I'll often rely on finding an interesting piece of driftwood to get my wheels turning. In this carving, the driftwood got me going, and with my fish pattern and a study cast, I was able to make several decisions on composition and design before I finished rough cutting.

1. I've found an interesting piece of driftwood, and I've chosen my pattern. I have also rough cut my fish from jelu-tong, and have begun to conceptualize my carving.

2. Here I've set up my compo-sition. The fish has been roughed out on the bandsaw. The driftwood in back has been cut and positioned and a second piece cut and laid on the base foreground. The nine-inch circle was cut from particle board shelving. The edges were cut off by tilting the bandsaw table. The fish has been connected to the driftwood with a ¼-inch rod.

3. The particle board base is then rounded and roughed up with a large carbide ball. I like particle board because it leaves a nondirectional texture.

4. This photo shows the driftwood attached and filled at its seam with the particle board base. The ¼-inch rod is also attached, covered with Bondo, and shaped as a branch. The fish's fins have been rough shaped. The dorsal and anal fin spines have been inserted with the grain running in the direction of the spines. The head structure and the pectoral fin girdle have been cut in with a small carbide drum.

5. Using my pattern and a study cast of a bluegill, I begin roughing in the facial contours. The fiberglass study cast is an excellent reference aid, actually better than keeping a frozen fish, since the surface contours and details can be clearly seen. Frozen specimens will freezer-burn eventually and are always a bit of a mess on a workbench.

63

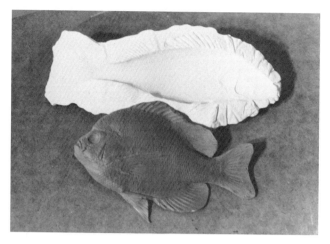

6. This photo shows my blue-gill study cast and a plaster mold of a yellow perch. A fiberglass study cast will be made of the yellow perch from the plaster mold. Getting good sharp crisp details in a cast is not as simple as pouring plaster over a fish. Since I specialized in fiberglass fish reproductions as a taxidermist for many years, I learned many tricks and steps for re-producing a fish in fiberglass accurately.

7. The fish has now been sanded with 60-grit sandpaper. The fin rays have also been cut with a carbide disk.

8. Using a diamond drum, I cut in the mouth structure, separate the opercular bones, and cut in the branchiostegal rays. I also define each spine in the dorsal and anal fins.

9. With a small ruby ball, I begin carving in the facial details and scales. I can easily copy these from my study cast and thereby eliminate any guesswork. The head of the fish is the most important area. Make an effort to capture the subtleties and character of the species. Carving in all this detail is what really makes a large-scaled fish turn out so well.

10. I cut in the lateral line with a cylindrical stone. Two cuts, one on each side of the line, leave a thin raised vein. Then I pencil in some directional guidelines for my scaling.

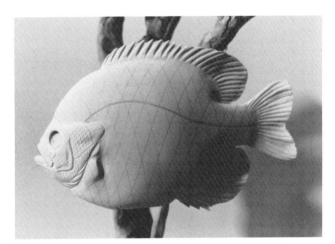

11. Diagonal scale lines are cut in one direction with a small ruby ball. Take care to keep the spaces consistent. I notice size changes at the caudal peduncle, breast, and forehead in my study cast. I make sure to copy them.

12. The second set of diagonal scale lines is cut in the opposite direction. This leaves a diamond-shaped grid pattern over the fish.

13. Using the same ruby ball, I carve in a crescent at the back of each diamond. This gives me my individually shaped scale. Notice the difference in the forehead above the gill flap. This area is not yet scale cut.

14. This photo shows the fish with the scaling completed.

15. After scaling, I turn my attention to the fins again. Notice the dorsal and anal fin spines. Accurate sharpness is achieved by inserting these parts with the grain going in their direction for strength. The soft rayed fins are detailed using the "whole, two-third, one-third" rule as in the brown trout.

16. The fins are cut out. Notice the thickness and the arrows indicating the direction of the grain. The fins are carved in the same manner as in the brown trout. Slots are cut and they are inserted. The eyes are also set. The fish is finished in the carving stage.

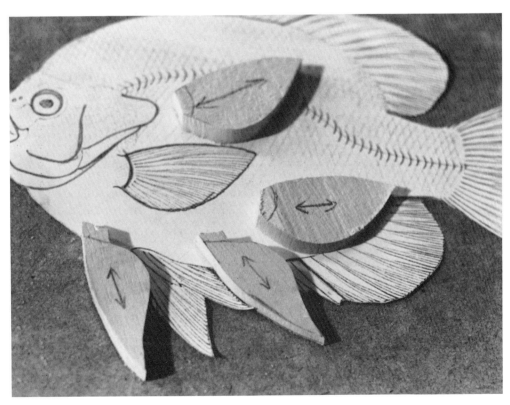

17. I turn my attention back to my base. My driftwood had one branch about ten to twelve inches—too tall—so I cut it off.

18. I cut the branch at an angle and drilled and set in a ¼-inch dowel.

19. The natural tip end was cut at an angle and drilled to fit the dowel.

20. I attached and filled the tip with Bondo. It was then detailed in a wide seam.

21. The fish and base are both finished and ready to paint.

22. Front view of fish.

23. Front quarter view of fish.

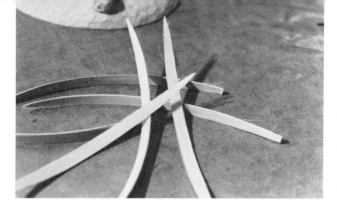

24. Making aquatic plants can be quite time-consuming. For this carving, I wanted to bring up some color and fill some of the base area. I decided to use split bamboo. I cut and shape individual leaves on my belt sander. Many stringy fibers remain and they are difficult to sand off. I use a butane torch to burn them off.

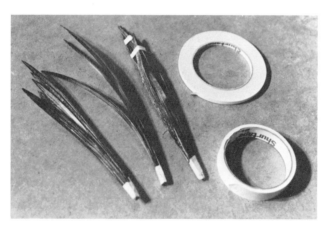

25. This photo shows the leaves after burning. Notice the texture of the bamboo.

26. After taping four or five leaves together at the base, I run them under a faucet to dampen the bundle. Then I twist and weave the leaves about one another and tape the tips together.

27. This photo shows three bundles twisted and taped. They are then set aside to dry.

Painting: The bluegill, like most fish, varies in color depending on its habitat, the season of the year, and its size, among other things. With that in mind, I usually choose a typical color phase that is appropriate for all areas rather than a local variation.

28. After sealing the wood, I went directly to my base colors. I used Neutral Gray value 3.0 for the back and upper fins and Neutral Gray value 7.0 for the belly and lower fins, blending the two at the transition area of the dark back and side at the lateral line.

29. Using Ivory Black, darken all upper fin bases, the upper back and the head. Then stipple in the vertical bars and darken the edges of the dorsal fins and tail. Dry brush across the spines and rays of the dorsal fins and tail.

30. Use Neutral Gray value 8.0 to lighten the fin edges of all the lower fins, then lighten the lower belly area also. At this point, I've established base values from light to dark over which thinner washes of color will be applied.

31. Using Vivid Red Orange, paint the breast, fading out at the pectoral fin and going as far back as the anal fin. Use very little paint and a fairly dry brush.

32. The next color is Cadmium Red Light. Use this mainly in the triangular area of the breast in front of the pectoral and pelvic fins. Fade quickly beyond this point. Use a dry brush and very little paint. The idea is to deepen the orange color at the front of the breast.

33. Mix Chromium Oxide Green, Neutral Gray value 4.0, and Iridescent Gold in about equal parts. Use this as a wash over the entire fish. Keep it thin over the orange breast. Then pick up more paint and darken the upper part of the fish. You're working more paint into the still-wet wash. This allows you to blend and pull as much color down the side of the fish as you want. Varying the amount of green, gold, and gray also helps to achieve variety and depth.

34. Dry brush Iridescent White on the lower portion of the caudal peduncle. Bring it forward over the orange, blending out towards the pectoral fin and up the side a little. Dry brush the lower face area also.

35. Lightly dry brush Iridescent Gold over the side of the fish and up onto the back to highlight scale detail. Carry this across the side of the face also.

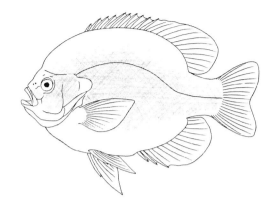

Finishing: Using Ivory Black again, repaint and darken the back and the vertical bars, fins, and so on.

Give the entire fish a thin wash of Raw Umber. This earthy brown will tone down the green, gold, orange, and pale fin edges and pull all the colors together.

Now it's time to attend to individual area details. Use Neutral Gray value 8.0 to lighten the lower fin margins, anal fin spines, and membrane areas around the mouth and gills. Use a mixture of Neutral Gray value 8.0, Chromium Oxide Green, and a bit of Raw Umber to lighten the membrane areas between the dorsal fin spines and rays, and the tail. Use Ivory Black and Ultramarine Blue to paint the blue gill flap. This should finish the painting.

Paint the base with Chromium Oxide Green, Raw Umber, Neutral Gray value 4.0, and Ivory Black. I work all the colors straight from the tube with only enough water to wet the bristles of my brush before I start. Working wet on wet, I paint a blended camouflage pattern, darker around the edges of the driftwood. When this is done, I blow it dry and then dry brush a light Neutral Gray over it, very light and very dry. The Bondo is painted to blend with the driftwood. Then the entire base is given a Raw Umber/Chromium Oxide Green wash. This blends the base into the driftwood. The plant leaves are painted with the Chromium Oxide Green, then lightly dry brushed with Bronze Yellow near the tips. Holes are drilled and the leaves are bundled and set in a two-part epoxy putty. Surface holdfast roots were modeled with the epoxy putty also. I had a very little ball of epoxy left over so I modeled a small snail and put it in. The roots and snail can be painted even before the epoxy is cured.

I chose teak for the base because it complements the orange in the fish and contrasts well with the greens. I turn all my own round bases on a lathe. This way, I can make sure the base, not only in color but also in shape, complements the rest of the piece.

7

Largemouth Bass

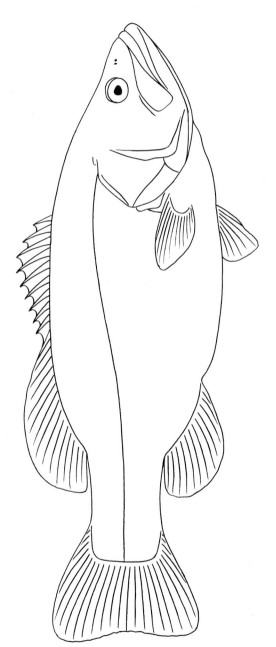

About the Pattern: The largemouth bass for this book project was carved from the same pattern as my 1986 World Championship piece, a large-mouth bass that placed not only First in the World Game Fish, but also Best in the World Freshwater Fish Carving.

My plan for the World Championship bass was simply to carve a fish doing what it does most of the time— hanging around, waiting for some unsuspecting meal to pass by. Its animation was pretty still, with only slight fin movement. I indicated the water surface with lily pads and paint on a submerged log. With the carving shown in this book, I wanted to give the fish a little more animation and interest. I altered the pattern by tip-ping up the caudal peduncle a little, opening up the fins a little more, and dropping the mouth open to add an attitude to the fish. The pattern for the turtle is an actual specimen.

Carving: My job as a wildlife artist is not merely to make a bunch of fish carvings. It is to tell a story or give an account of nature so the viewer understands exactly what is going on. I use some artistic license, but rely mostly on nature's examples to present an accurate picture. In this carving, I achieve accuracy in shape and texture with the Foredom tool and with hand tools.

1. The basic design was set up using lots of driftwood tangle, and the bass and a turtle. The bass has been rough-sawed on the bandsaw and the dorsal and anal fins have been inserted. The turtle has been positioned swimming around and under the driftwood. The driftwood has been cut, glued, screwed, and filled to the free-form particle board base.

2. This photo shows the head structure cut in, and the visceral dip and tail base cut with the fins thinned.

3. The head details are blended with a chisel and the visceral dip is tapered out also.

4. After sanding with 60-grit sandpaper, I sketch in head details. Then they're cut in with a ruby ball.

5. The head details are sanded and blended with sanding screen. The lateral line has been cut in.

6. The fin rays are then cut in with a carbide disk. Notice the curve to each individual ray.

7. Scaling is started. Cut the scales on the first diagonal with a small ruby ball.

8. Cutting on the opposite diagonal with a small ruby ball leaves a diamond grid pattern.

9. Now make a third cut with the same ruby ball, taking off the back corner of the diamond shape. This leaves a rounded scale.

10. The eyes are set at this point, and the spiny first dorsal is inserted. Since the spines are so sharp and thus fragile, I waited until the fish was scale detailed before installing the first dorsal.

11. The fin pairs are carved and inserted into slots with Bondo.

12. The finished carving is ready to seal and paint.

13. Detail of opposite side. Notice the mouth, slightly open, and the shape of the pectoral fin. The fish is attached by a ¼-inch rod at the caudal peduncle. It seems framed from the angled rear shot and floats over the driftwood from the front.

14. The turtle specimen for this carving is a small freeze-dried turtle I bought at a taxidermy competition a few years ago. The pattern is the actual turtle. This photo shows the turtle and the top view of the shell cut out.

15. The top of the shell is chip-carved to a rough shape. Notice the centerline and the edge line.

16. The bottom of the shell is then chip-carved.

17. A few minutes with my Foredom and a small carbide ball distinguish the soft skin areas from the shell edges.

18. After a quick sanding with 60-grit paper, the individual plates are penciled in.

19. The plates are burned in with a hot tip. This will help me keep these edges while I carve each plate.

20. Using a diamond cylinder, I lower the edges of each plate at the burned-in guideline.

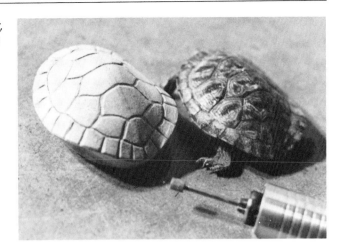

21. Then I carve in the texture and soften the edges of each plate with a small ruby ball.

22. The bottom of the shell has a softer, smooth look and feel to it.

23. The legs, head, and tail were carved separately and installed with epoxy putty.

24. The top front view showing the finished turtle carving, ready to paint. The eye and other minute details will be painted in.

25. The turtle as it will be positioned on the carving. It actually has an S-curve to it. The head is angled to one side and up and the tail is curved to the other side and down, creating a flow of motion.

Painting: The painting of the largemouth bass is very much like painting the blue-gill in the previous chapter. Establish a paint schedule, and rely on your reference photos for accuracy of color and pattern.

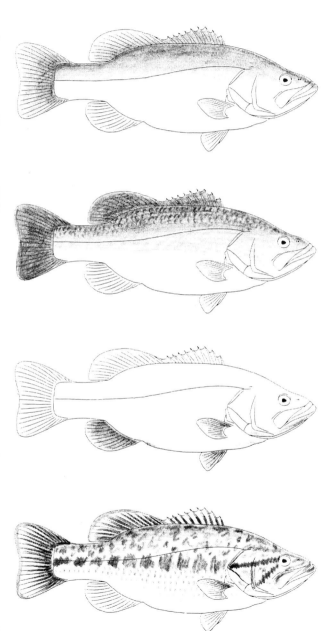

26. Use Neutral Gray value 7.0 on the fish's belly and side, including the tail. Then use Neutral Gray value 4.0 on the back. Dry brush this down over the lighter value (7.0). Paint the base of the tail, then pick up some water and blend the paint out to the edge.

The next four colors are Iridescent White, Silver, Gold, and Bronze. Paint these in order from the belly up. Blend the transition areas wet on wet as you work from the white on the belly to the bronze on the back.

27. Paint the back and upper fins with a medium wash of Iridescent Bronze and Chromium Oxide Green. Blow it dry and then dry brush over the same area, dragging down and fading out past the lateral line.

28. Using Light Magenta, paint the pelvic and anal fins. Add a thin wash on the pectoral fin. Put a little on the lower jaw area and the vent as well.

Using a medium wash, paint Raw Sienna on all the fins, thinner on the pelvic and anal fin.

29. With Ivory Black, dry brush the back and the upper fins. Dry brush/stipple in the mottled markings.

The next step is to dry brush Iridescent Gold over the back and down the side.

83

Finishing: With a fat-tipped gold-paint marking pen, scale the back and side down to the belly. Skip some scales, especially on the black patterns. After this is dry, tone down the center back with a dry brushing of Ivory Black and then a wash of Chromium Oxide Green and Raw Umber. Tone down the markings but don't paint them out. Go very lightly with the dry brush and use a very thin wash.

The black markings are then redone scale by scale with a small brush and Ivory Black, Chromium Oxide Green, and Iridescent Bronze all mixed together, heavy on the black.

At this point, I paint the light skin membrane areas around the mouth and head with white. Lighten the lower fin edges with a dry brushing of white also.

Continue painting and redoing areas until you're satisfied. When the fish is finished, give it a couple coats of high gloss lacquer and attach it permanently to the base.

The painting of the turtle is just as time-consuming as painting the bass, because of all the detail and small lines on a small carving. Use your reference materials to get the colors right.

The overall carving implies a multitude of scenarios between the bass and the turtle. I'm sure each viewer will imagine his own outcome.

8

Lionfish and Queen Angelfish

About the Pattern: This particular carving is a commissioned piece that happened in perfect timing for this book. I was given basic guidelines for a lionfish and queen angelfish composition on one base, and a Plexiglas case to protect it and keep it dust free.

To begin the project, I went to my files and found my lionfish pattern and some photo reference. I also went through my books and found a few more helpful photos. My lionfish pattern is a combination of studies made at Seaworld, San Diego; Scripps Aquarium, La Jolla; and my photo references. I might add here that there are several different types of lionfish. This one is the species *volitans*. Also a point to note is that fish continue to grow until they die. Larger fish are generally older fish. Lionfish are no exception. Besides the obvious size differences, older fish have larger pectoral fins and facial skin flaps.

The queen angelfish was drawn from a specimen given to me by an aquarist. I maintain contact with private and public aquariums and obtain specimens when they die.

The banded butterfly fish was added to set the scene. I needed a fish for the back (or nonshow) side of the carving. It was designed from several photos and my knowledge of other butterfly fishes.

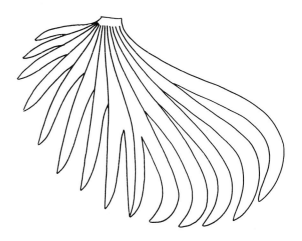

Carving: The fishes' bodies will be carved from jelutong, but the lionfish's fins will be cut from Plexiglas and inserted. I'll use the bandsaw, hand tools, burner, and power tools—and toothpicks. The angelfish carving is a little more conventional. The base will be cut from clear pine, and the habitat pieces will be carved from bandsaw scraps. The whole thing must fit in a twenty-four-inch Plexiglas case.

1. This photo shows my pattern and selected photo references.

2. The body is rough-cut just as with all other fish. All the fins will be made out of Plexiglas and inserted. The fins have been traced on the Plexiglas's protective paper.

3. The head structure details are cut in.

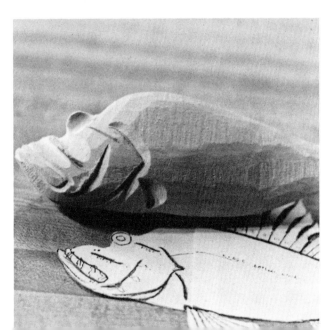

4. The head is shaped and sanded. Notice the raised lateral line.

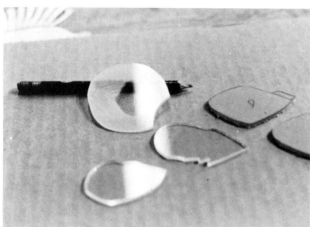

5. The fins are cut from the Plexiglas. The fins in the foreground have the protective paper removed. The tail, lying on the pencil, has been thinned around the edges on my belt sander.

6. This photo shows the second dorsal, caudal, and anal fins sanded and thinned to their edges on both sides.

7. The fin rays are penciled right on the fins by simply placing the Plexiglas fins over the pattern.

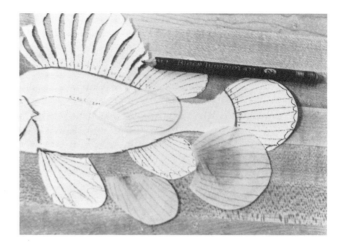

8. The fin rays are then ground in with a carbide disk.

9. Using a propane torch, I heat both sides of the fins, then carefully bend and shape them as they cool. I hold the fins in a spring clamp. Be careful not to burn the Plexiglas, as it will bubble and discolor. Most of the tooling and sanding marks will melt out and the fins will become clearer.

10. The fins are held in a spring clamp. Notice the bent-in shape.

11. This photo shows the centerline fins installed. Notice that the first dorsal has not been heated and bent yet. I find it easier to do this fin after it's been set in the fish. Also note its opaque look compared to the other fins. The pelvic fins are carved, ready to be heated and installed. The body is then scale-textured with a ruby ball.

12. Holes are drilled for spine inserts.

13. Sharpened toothpicks are set in epoxy putty and blended into the fish.

14. Now I paint the clear flint eye blanks. Using Ivory Black, Burnt Umber, Raw Sienna, and Titanium White, I paint the patterns that run through the eyes. I use Ivory Black for the pupil, then Raw Sienna for the bars and Burnt Umber to edge the bars. White then covers the back.

15. When the eyes are thoroughly dry, they can be set in. The pelvic fins are also installed at this point. The dorsal fin has been heated and every other spine bent from side to side.

16. Detail of first spiny dorsal and alternate right-left tilt of spines.

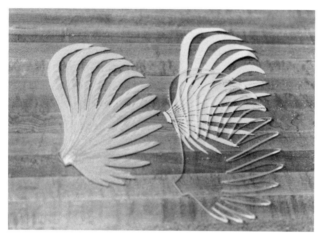

17. The pectoral fins are cut out on the bandsaw. It's not practical to thin the edges on the belt sander. This must be done as you work each individual fin ray. This photo shows the clear fin blank, the pattern, and a carved, or ground, fin.

18. This photo shows the ground fin. Notice the wavy thinness ground into each fin ray. The pectorals can then be heated and bent into shape.

19. For the lionfish facial flaps, I use manila folders. Small pieces are cut and glued into slots burned into the fish at the proper place and angle.

20. When the glue has dried, I burn the flaps to proper shape with my burner on high. Watch for small embers. Check the pectoral fins for proper fit. The lionfish is now ready to paint. The pectoral fins are painted and installed after the body has been painted.

21. The queen angelfish is cut out and rough-shaped on the bandsaw.

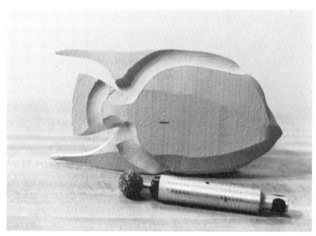

22. With a 1-inch carbide ball, I establish the fin bases. Cut in until the bases are about ⅜-inch thick. The little dark line is one of the imperfections that can appear in jelutong. I don't worry about them.

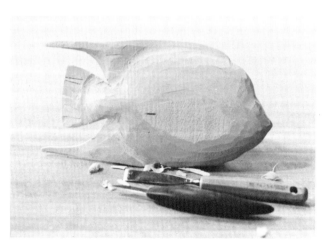

23. With a knife and ½-inch chisel, I flatten out and blend these grooves into the fish's body and roughly thin the fins. Notice that the flat bandsawed area on the side has been reduced substantially. This will eventually be worked from the operculars and pectoral fin area also. I'll end up without any flat area on the side.

24. With a ¼-inch carbide cylinder, cut in the head detail lines and the pectoral fin girdle. I've also thinned the edges of the fins and established the caudal peduncle.

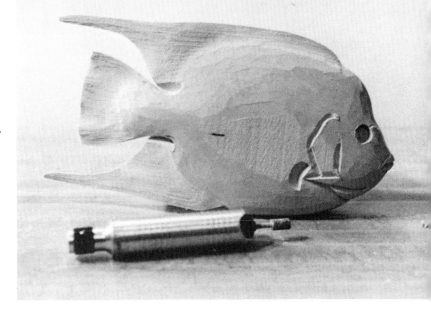

25. Back to knife and chisel to taper the previous cuts. Notice the bandsawed side area. It's almost gone, since the entire side of the fish has been shaped.

26. Sand and blend the fish with 60-grit sandpaper.

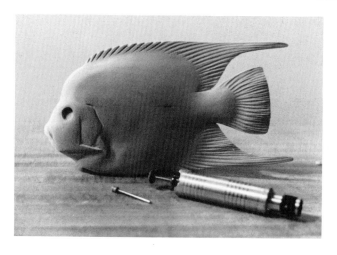

27. The fin rays are cut in. Use a diamond cylinder for sharp spines and a carbide disk for the soft rays.

28. I switch to a larger ruby ball and soften all the fin rays.

29. With a small ruby ball, I carve in a scale grid pattern over the body. Notice how the scales run out over the fin rays.

30. Using the same ruby ball, I round off the back of each diamond, forming an individual scale. The back half of the fish has been scale cut; the front half from the ruby ball forward has not been completed. The difference is apparent. Individual scaling is worth the time and effort involved.

31. The head and face are finished with texturing. Notice the random squibbly-type texture on the face, and the spines on the operculum.

32. The whole fish has been scaled. It's ready for fin pairs and eyes.

33. Profile of finished fish; eyes and fin pairs have been added.

34. Front view. Notice the sculptural natural curves from the dorsal fin to the forehead, eye, face and on down to the pelvic fins.

35. Reverse side of finished fish. Notice how the imperfection has been filled and textured. The fish is now complete and ready for painting.

36. The base was cut from ⁵⁄₄-inch clear pine in a hexagon shape. Additional pieces were cut free-form with multiple curves and angles, and glued into place. This roughed-out base structure begins my "stacking" arrangement.

37. Using my Auto Mach power wood carver, I gouge out and blend the bandsawed cuts.

38. With my bandsaw, Bondo, and odd-shaped scraps, I set up a branching coral head. Each branch was roughed out and glued up with Bondo. I use ¼-inch dowels to hold everything together as I arrange my coral. In this carving, I had to stay inside a vertical line around the base, since it will be enclosed in the custom Plexiglas case.

39. With a mallet and a 1-inch chisel, I taper and slope the front of the base down to about ¼ inch. This totally removes the flat surface of the top of the pine baseboard. I've left a flat area to the right where I'll add something. Notice the ¼-inch dowel where the coral head will sit.

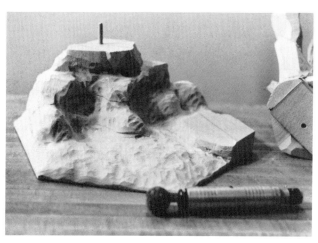

40. Working quickly with a 1-inch carbide ball, I round off the chisel and gouge cuts.

41. The branching staghorn coral head is rough-shaped with a large carbide ball. Fire coral is added to the right and sponges to the left. The mound at the lower right will be a fungus coral.

42. The sponges and the fungus coral have been shaped and attached. A bit of leaf coral in the foreground has also been carved in.

43. Positioning of the queen angelfish. One-fourth-inch threaded rod has been secured in the coral head. The fish was drilled between the pelvic fins. The rod was bent in a vise and vise grips before installation. It was bent and fit several times until the positioning was exact. Notice the extended tape checking the height. The carving must fit in an already ordered 24-inch-high custom Plexiglas case.

44. The lionfish has been installed for test fit.

45. The overall composition is checked. The lionfish fits under the coral head and touches at only a single inconspicuous ¼-inch connection near the base of the tail.

46. This photo shows the base without the fish. The sponges, fire coral, and fungus coral have been given a stippled texture of 50–50 modeling paste and gesso. The staghorn coral was textured with a small carbide ball.

Painting: Painting the lionfish is actually quite simple. It's the queen angelfish that gets complicated. After the lionfish is painted, I can tackle the angelfish.

47. The body of the lionfish is given one or two coats of gesso and then a coat of Titanium White. The fin rays and spines are also painted white, both sides. This must be done with care, since the thin membrane areas should remain clear. After the white has been painted, I repaint the body with a coat of Iridescent White. This gives the body a pearly look.

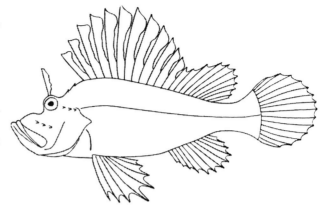

48. Using Burnt Umber, I paint in all the barred markings on the body and fins. I paint the wide bars first and then the smaller ones in between. I try to keep the markings similar on each side, connecting over the head, back, tail, and belly. Don't forget to do the facial skin flaps. At this point, the two-color fish should be looking pretty good.

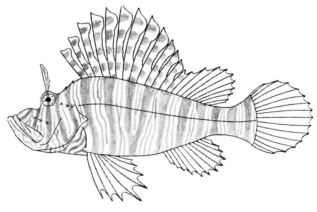

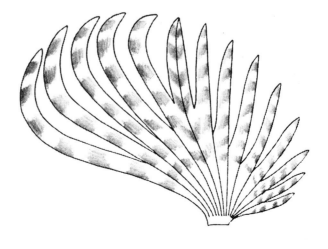

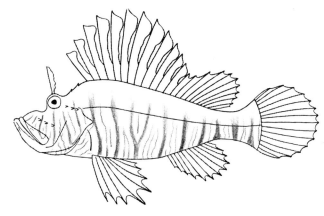

49. I now use Raw Sienna and Iridescent Gold mixed together and add in the lighter tones in the wide bars. I bring this up from the belly and let it fade out between the lateral line and the dorsal fins. Keep this color inside the Burnt Umber, so there's a dark edge on either side of the bar. Remember the facial skin flaps.

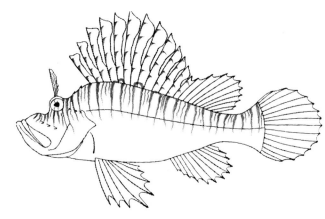

50. Once this is done, I come back the other way with Burnt Umber and Ivory Black, using a fine liner, and darken the wide bars at their edges down to about the lateral line. I also darken the smaller lines and bars on the upper tail, back, and head. That's about it for the lionfish. The brown barring on the pectoral fins is dry brushed in on both sides. This helps give a soft blended look rather than sharply defined markings.

51. The queen angelfish is more time-consuming and tedious to paint than the lion-fish. I paint it one side at a time to get the base back-ground colors on and blended in one operation. I put Payne's Gray, Cerulean Blue, Brilliant Blue Purple, Ivory Black, Prism Violet, Chromium Oxide Green, and Turner's Yellow on my palette. I start by painting the tail, pectoral fins, pelvic fins, and the side of the face with Turner's Yellow, two coats to cover if necessary.

52. Then I begin painting the rest of the fish with Payne's Gray as my first undercoat. Paint this everywhere and while it is still wet, add in the Cerulean Blue and Brilliant Blue Purple on the lower part of the body, blending wet on wet.

53. I now go to the Chromium Oxide Green and work it in from the dorsal fin down the back to the yellow on the face, blending and stippling wet on wet. Do not paint out the yellow. If the yellow in the face starts getting too green, pick up some more yellow and bring it back in to the green. When the entire side has been painted and blended, blow it dry and paint the other side exactly the same. (Easier said than done!)

54. With the base colors in, I then start dry brushing the Brilliant Blue Purple around the facial areas, the "crown," and dorsal and anal fin edges. Blow this dry and do it a second time with a little Titanium White added. Dry brush this over the straight color so as not to repaint all the blue completely. This adds depth and interest to the blue markings.

55. Paint the inside of the crown with Ivory Black mixed with a little Prism Violet. Also use this to paint the dark spot at the base of the pectoral fins. The blue edge on the dorsal and anal fins is separated by a thin black line also. This turns into a purplish-blue spot just above and below the caudal peduncle on each fin. I paint this spot with the Prism Violet and Brilliant Blue Purple. Blow this dry and add in the purple center on the spot at the base of the pectoral fin.

56. Now, using a small round-pointed brush, paint in the yellow scale markings on each side. I use Turner's Yellow and a little gesso to help make it opaque. I paint one diagonal row at a time. These markings are larger on the middle side of the fish and smaller into the dorsal and anal fins as well as into the forehead. They fade out at a line from the pectoral fin to the anal fin. I usually paint these scale markings three or four times. Each time, my brush strokes improve and correct the pattern. Consider that you have to paint both sides three to four times; allow plenty of time and don't rush it.

Finishing: I finish up the angelfish with Brilliant Yellow Green washes on the yellow fins. Then I dry brush and paint the elongated dorsal and anal fin tips with Turner's Yellow. I add in and blend Cadmium Red Light and Yellow Orange Azo at the top of the dorsal fin and bottom of the anal fin. At this point it's just a matter of refining individual areas. This is the type of fish that you could paint on forever. (I paint them till they're done.) I've got dozens of reference pictures of queen angels and every one is a little different.

Painting the base is always fun for me. I put dozens of colors on my palette and try to use them all. I repeat every color that I've used in the fish, except the iridescents, plus others to complement and some to accent. I paint my bases very much like I paint the base colors of the queen angel. I use two or three colors wet on wet to paint most of the parts. My main objective is to get the paint into all of the texture and detail without excess buildup. I work quite fast to get the paint on. Then I blow it dry, and dry brush and wash individual areas for details.

9

Gallery

Rainbow trout.

Brown trout.

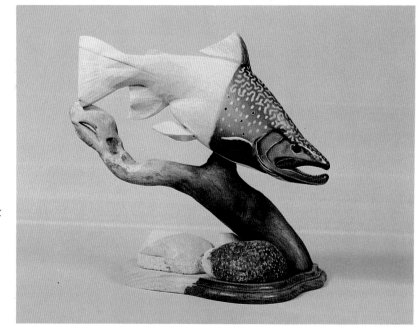

Brook trout.

Above left, lionfish and queen angelfish; above right, queen angelfish, detail; below left, lionfish, detail; below right, bluegill.

Largemouth bass
and turtle.

*"La Jolla Cove
Special"*: garibaldi
with purple urchin
and wavy turban.

*Redbreast sunfish.
Second place: Fresh-
water Single Fish,
1987 World
Championships.*

Garibaldi, detail.

ED MILLER

*Brown
bullhead
catfish.*

113

Rainbow trout. Best in the World Trout, 1986 World Championships.

Snake River cutthroat trout, detail.

Snake River cutthroat trout. Second in the World: Trouts and Salmon, 1987 World Championships of Freshwater Fish Carving.

MICHAEL SCHEAR

Sea run steelhead trout.

Bottom left, five reef fish: lionfish, naso tang, emperor angelfish, clown triggerfish, zebra moray. Above, five reef fish details.

Above, gray angelfish composition carved for Vice President George Bush in 1987. Right, gray angelfish composition, detail.

Above, rainbow trout pair.

Right, small-mouth bass. 1988 Second in the World Fresh-water Fish Group.

Red-tailed
butterfly fish.

*Left, large-
mouth bass.
World
Champion
Freshwater
Fish, 1986.
Above right,
largemouth
bass, detail.*

119

The author's first
decorative fish
carving: a moorish
idol and a female
bird wrasse, with
natural coral.
Property of Wildlife
World Museum,
Monument, Colorado.

Ornate butterfly
fish and tiger
cowrie. World
Champion Fish
Carving, 1985.

Wrase 3"L *3/4"H

Above, bonefish and blue crab with oysters. Third in the World Saltwater Fish, 1987.

Angled arrangement: black crappie trio. 1988 First in the World Freshwater Fish Group.

Baja California reef composition: king angelfish and banded butterfly fish with black murex, sea fan, and red sea urchin.

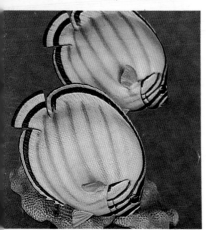

ED MILLER

Top left,
Christmas
wrasse and
Triton's
trumpet;
bottom left,
ornate
butterfly
fish pair;
right, bandit
angelfish.

ED MILLER

Above left, raccoon butterfly fish; above right, cortez angelfish, adult and juvenile; below right, queen angelfish.

ED MILLER

ED MILLER

ED MILLER

Above left, yellow-headed wrasse; above right, Hawaiian sergeant major; below left, clown triggerfish; below right, garibaldi and black abalone.

2

Additional Patterns

Ornate Butterfly Fish

The ornate butterfly fish is a favorite
fish of mine. It's found in Hawaiian
waters. Most of the time, you'll
see ornate butterfly fish in pairs,
since they mate for life.

The pattern was drawn from a
collected specimen.

This is the fish I carved for my entry in
the 1985 World Championships.

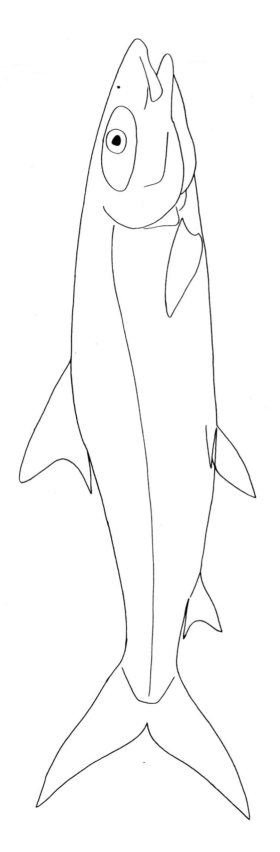

Bonefish

The "silver bullet" of the saltwater flats is renowned for its angling and fighting tenacity.

The pattern was drawn directly from a fish collected in Florida. All the fins are inserted.

This fish placed third for saltwater fish at the 1987 World Championships.

Red-tailed Butterfly Fish

This beautiful fish from the Indian Ocean caught my eye at a large exhibit at Sea World, San Diego, where it was part of a display.

The pattern was developed through observation and direct color notes.

To carve this fish, follow the steps in carving the queen angelfish in Chapter 8.

Garibaldi

The garibaldi is a Southern California favorite. It's completely protected from fishing, but you can easily observe one by snorkeling or diving in shallow rocky areas. Simply break open a sea urchin, and dozens of garibaldi will swarm around.

The pattern was developed from photo references and observation of live specimens.

The body is bright orange and the eyes are a brilliant blue green, as shown in the color plate.

Redbreast Sunfish

The redbreast sunfish won second place, freshwater single fish at the 1987 World Championships. It was done using the same steps as for the bluegill in this book, Chapter 6.

The pattern was drawn from a fiberglass reproduction.

The green of the plants worked quite well in color contrast with the red-orange breast of the sunfish (see color plate).

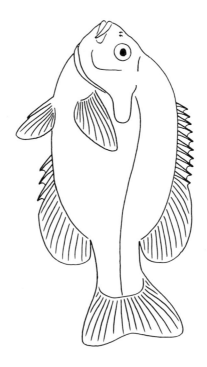

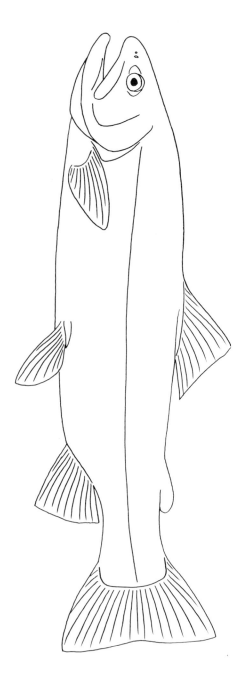

Snake River Cutthroat Trout

The specimen for this pattern was brought to me with great care by my friend Jim Kermot. He caught the fish in a small stream near Jackson, Wyoming. I had asked him to save one with good body conformation. Cutthroat trout are found in deep holes and undercut banks in their small-stream habitat.

Carve this fish as you would the brown trout in Chapter 4.

The presentation of this fish is quite different from most of my other compositions. The planning and execution of the base involved more work than my normal free-form or round presentation. It was worth the effort, though, since this composition was awarded Second in the World, Trouts in 1987.

Brown Bullhead Catfish

Although not the prettiest fish one can think of, the catfish can be very interesting as a carving. The pattern was drawn from a specimen caught by my four-year-old son.

All the fins except the tail were added or inserted. The whiskers are tapered wires, epoxied in and bent to shape. The texture was two coats of stippled modeling paste and gesso mixed 50–50. This gives a smooth but dimpled texture to the body. Use only gesso on the fins to preserve the detail.

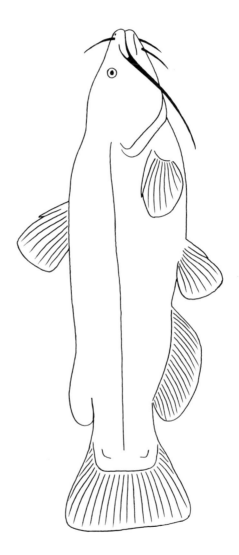

Black Crappie

The pattern for my black crappie was drawn from a fiberglass reproduction I had done when I had my taxidermy studio.

Carve the crappie using the steps outlined in the largemouth bass chapter (Chapter 7).

My crappie compositions are based on angles. This triple crappie composition won Best in the World Panfish in 1987.

Afterword

The future for fish carving looks very bright. Interest in carving fish is growing rapidly. Many carvers are trying a fish or two and finding new satisfaction and new challenges. As more carvers do fish, they naturally look for shows and competitions where they can display and compete. Some wildfowl shows have been quick to recognize this and have already added fish carving categories to their shows (See Appendix for listing.).

The fish carvings do not take away from the wildfowl carvings. They add a great deal of interest, especially for the viewing public. I expect some other shows and festivals will add fish carvings as interest grows.

Many taxidermy competitions will generally accept wood carvings under their reproduction categories for fish. This was my first and only option with my first few fish carvings. The main problem here is that the carver competes against compositions made of both natural and reproduced parts.

Another area of concern for contests is the use of nonwood items in compositions. For example, Plexiglas is often used for fins. Carvers also use paper, epoxies, and thin metals such as copper, brass, and aluminum. Should competitive carvings be allowed to contain such materials? Show committees must address this problem. Also to be considered are the nonwood items often used in

bases. Plastic aquarium plants, commercially made lily pads and flowers, natural sand, pebbles, and rocks have already made judging a little difficult when rules do not prohibit these items.

My personal point of view is two-pronged. On the one hand, competitions should set down some general and some specific rules, and make it perfectly clear what is or is not acceptable in their fish carving competitions. Initially, shows and competitions have limited categories and rules. This changes yearly as more carvings of all types of fish are brought to shows. The rules will be expanded and refined as time goes on. Show committees should be careful, though, that they don't allow so many refinements that the rules become confusing.

On the other hand, as an artist, I do not want my work to be restricted by a long list of dos and don'ts for someone else's convenience. I enjoy a wonderful freedom to do things the way I want to do them. My creative ideas and impulses are not limited to the criteria demanded by competition committees or restrictive rules. It's nice to win awards and competitions but it matters very little to some galleries and patrons. If it sells, it's a winner by a completely different set of rules.

Bibliography

Boom, Robert. *Hawaiian Seashells*. The Waikiki Association, 1972.

Brooks, Joe. *Trout Fishing*. An Outdoor Life Book. Harper and Row, 1972.

Campbell, Andrew C. *Life in the Sea*. Hamlyn, 1978.

———. *Seashore Life*. Exeter Books, 1983.

Cousteau, Jacques-Yves. *Jacques Cousteau: The Ocean World*. Harry N. Abrams, Inc., 1985.

Cousteau, Jacques-Yves, and Philippe Diole. *Life and Death in a Coral Sea*. Doubleday and Company, Inc., 1971.

Cousteau, Jacques-Yves, and Thomas H. Suchanek. *Marine Life of the Caribbean*. Skyline Press, 1984.

Elman, Robert. *The Fisherman's Field Guide*. Alfred A. Knopf, 1977.

Farrington, S. Kip Jr. *Pacific Game Fishing*. Coward-McCann, Inc., 1942.

Faulkner, Douglas, and Lavett C. Smith. *The Hidden Sea*. Viking Press, 1970.

Fielding, Ann. *Hawaiian Reefs and Tidepools*. Oriental Publishing Company, 1982.

Gosline, William A., and Vernon E. Brock. *Handbook of Hawaiian Fishes*. University of Hawaii Press, 1960.

Gotshall, Daniel W. *Fishwatcher's Guide to the Inshore Fishes of the Pacific Coast*. Sea Challengers, 1977.

Greenberg, Idaz, and Jerry Greenberg. *Guide to Corals and Fishes of Florida, The Bahamas, and the Caribbean*. Seahawk Press, 1977.

Heacox, Cecil E. *The Compleat Brown Trout*. Winchester Press, 1974.

Heilner, Van Campen. *Saltwater Fishing*. Alfred A. Knopf, 1953.

Herald, Earl S. *Living Fishes of the World*. Hamish Hamilton, 1961.

Herter, George Leonard. *Minnows of North America and their Streamer Imitations*. Herter's, Inc., 1971.

Hobson, Edmund, and E. H. Chave. *Hawaiian Reef Animals*. University Press of Hawaii, 1979.

Hubbs, Carl L., and Karl F. Lagler. *Fishes of the Great Lakes Region*. Cranbrook Institute of Science, 1952.

Humann, Paul. *Ocean Realm Guide to Corals of Florida, Bahamas and the Caribbean*. Ocean Realm Publishing Corporation, 1983.

Johnson, Scott. *Living Seashells*. Oriental Publishing Company, N.d.

La Gorce, John Oliver. *The Book of Fishes*. National Geographic Society, 1961.

Mason, Jerry. *The American Sportsman Treasury*. Alfred A. Knopf, 1971.

McClane, A. J. *McClane's New Standard Fishing Encyclopedia*. Holt, Rinehart and Winston, Inc., 1965.

———. *Field & Stream International Fishing Guide*. Holt, Rinehart and Winston, Inc., 1971.

———. *McClane's Field Guide to Freshwater Fishes of North America*. Holt, Rinehart and Winston, 1974.

———. *McClane's Field Guide to Salt-water Fishes of North America.* Holt, Rinehart and Winston, 1974.

Migdalski, Edward C. *How to Make Fish Mounts and Other Fish Trophies.* The Ronald Press Company, 1960.

Migdalski, Edward C., and George S. Fichter. *The Fresh and Salt Water Fishes of the World.* Alfred A. Knopf, 1976.

Miller, Daniel J., and Robert N. Lea. *Guide to the Coastal Marine Fishes of California.* State of California Department of Fish and Game, 1972.

Morris, Percy A. *A Field Guide to Shells of the Pacific Coast and Hawaii.* Houghton Mifflin Company, 1952.

Nayman, Jacqueline. *Whales, Dolphins and Man.* Hamlyn, 1973.

Randall, John E. *Underwater Guide to Hawaiian Reef Fishes.* Harrowood Books, 1981.

Reece, Maynard. *Fish and Fishing.* Meredith Press, 1963.

Rehder, Harald A. *The Audubon Society Field Guide to North American Seashells.* Alfred A. Knopf, 1981.

Roessler, Carl. *The Undersea Predators.* Facts on File Publications, 1984.

———. *Coral Kingdoms.* Harry N. Abrams, Inc., 1986.

Romashko, Sandra. *The Coral Book.* Windward Publishing, Inc., 1975.

———. *Living Coral.* Windward Publishing, Inc., 1976.

Sternberg, Dick. *The Art of Freshwater Fishing.* Publication Arts, Inc., 1982.

Swisher, Doug, and Carl Richards. *Fly Fishing Strategy.* Crown Publishers, Inc., 1975.

Thomson, Donald A., Lloyd T. Findley, and Alex N. Kerstitch. *Reef Fishes of the Sea of Cortez.* John Wiley & Sons, 1979.

Torchio, Menico. *The World Beneath the Sea.* Crown Publishers, Inc., 1974.

Van Gytenbeek, R. P. *The Way of a Trout.* J. B. Lippincott Company, 1972.

Walford, Lionel A. *Marine Game Fishes of the Pacific Coast from Alaska to the Equator.* University of California Press, Berkeley, 1937.

Walls, Jerry G. *Cowries.* T. F. H. Publications, Ltd., 1979.

Waterman, Charles F. *The Fisherman's World.* Random House, N.d.

———. *Fishing in America.* Holt, Rinehart and Winston, Inc. 1975.

Wheeler, Alwyne. *Fishes of the World: An Illustrated Dictionary.* Macmillan Publishing Co., Inc., 1975.

Woolner, Frank. *Modern Saltwater Sport Fishing.* Crown Publishers, Inc., 1972.

Appendices

Competitions Specifically for Fish Carvers

North American Wildfowl Carving
    Championship
    c/o Neal Stoneback
    12620 Southfield Road
    Detroit, MI 48223

    The Holiday Inn, Livonia, MI, is the
    site for this key show in late Septem-
    ber. Decorative fish carvings added in
    1987.

Racine Masters Carving Competition
    c/o Rick Beyer
    1115 North Main Street
    Racine, WI 53402

    Co-sponsored by Dremel Manufactur-
    ing and Ducks Unlimited. Held in
    late February. Wildfowl competition
    held in conjunction with fish carving
    competition. Multiple fish carving
    categories including freshwater, salt-
    water, and natural finish. Prize
    money.

World Championship Freshwater Fish
    Carving Contest
    c/o Jim Reynolds
    414 Emerson Road
    Traverse City, MI 49684

    Sponsored by Northwestern Michigan
    Waterfowl Decoy Association.
    Held in conjunction with a decoy
    contest and waterfowl art show in
    mid-October. Multiple freshwater fish
    categories. Prize money.

World Wildlife Art Festival
    1306 West Spring Street
    P.O. Box 967
    Monroe, GA 30655

    Sponsored by Wildlife Artist Supply
    Company and Breakthrough Publica-
    tions. Held in mid-August in Macon,
    GA. World championships for fish
    carvings including saltwater, fresh-
    water, and sculpture categories. Prize
    money.

Sources for Supplies

Materials and Tools

Al's Decoy Supplies
27 Connaught Ave.
London, Ontario N5Y 3A4
CANADA
519-451-4729

Albert Constantine & Sons,
  Inc.
2050 Eastchester Rd.
Bronx, NY 10461
212-792-1600

American Sales Co.
Box 741
Reseda, CA 91335
213-881-2808

Big Sky Carvers
8256 Huffine Ln.
Bozeman, MT 59715
406-586-0008

Buck Run Carvings
Box 151, Gully Rd.
Aurora, NY 13026
315-364-8414

Canadian Woodworker Ltd.
1391 St. James St.
Winnipeg, Manitoba
  R3H 0Z1
CANADA
204-786-3196

The Carver's Barn
P.O. Box 686
Rte. 28
Hearth & Eagle Shopping
  Plaza
South Yarmouth, MA 02664

Carvers Corner
153 Passaic St.
Garfield, NJ 07026
201-472-7511

Chez La Rogue
Rt. 3, Box 148
Foley, AL 36535
205-943-1237

Craft Cove, Inc.
2315 W. Glen Ave.
Peoria, IL 61614
309-692-8365

CraftWoods
10921 York Rd.
Cockeysville, MD 21030
301-667-9663

Curt's Waterfowl Corner
123 Le Boeuf St.
Montegut, LA 70377
504-594-3012

The Duck Butt Boys
P.O. Box 2051
Metairie, LA 70004
504-443-3797

Electric & Tool Service Co.
19442 Conant Ave.
Detroit, MI 48234
313-366-3830

P.C. English Enterprises
P.O. Box 7937
Lafayette Blvd.
Fredericksburg, VA 22404
703-371-1306

Exotic Woods Inc.
2483 Industrial Street
Burlington, Ontario
  L7P 1A6
CANADA
416-335-8066

Feather Merchants
279 Boston Post Rd.
Madison, CT 06443
203-245-1231

The Fine Tool Shops, Inc.
P.O. Box 1262
20 Backus Ave.
Danbury, CT 06810
800-243-1037

The Foredom Electric Co.
Rt. 6
Bethel, CT 06801
203-792-8622

Forest Products
P.O. Box 12
Avon, OH 44011
216-937-5630

Garrett Wade
161 Avenue of the Americas
New York, NY 10013
800-212-2942

Gerry's Tool Shed
1111 Flint Road
Unit 6
Downsview, Ontario
M3J 3C7
CANADA
416-665-6677

Gesswein
Woodworking Products
   Division
255 Hancock Ave.
P.O. Box 3998
Bridgeport, CT 06605
800-243-4466
203-366-5400

J. H. Kline Carving Shop
R.D. 2, Forge Hill Rd.
Manchester, PA 17345
717-266-3501

Ken Jones
P.O. Box 563
Salem, NH 03079

Kent's Woodshed
625 W. Main
Broussard, LA 70518
318-837-9470

Lee Valley Tools Ltd.
2680 Queensview Dr.
Ottawa, Ontario K2B 8J9
CANADA
613-596-0350

Lewis Tool and Supply Co.
912 West 8th St.
Loveland, CO 80537
303-663-4405

Little Mountain Carving
   Supply
Rt. 2, Box 1329
Front Royal, VA 22630
703-662-6160

L. I. Woodcarvers Supply
60 Glouster Rd.
Massapequa, NY 11758
516-799-7999

McGray Wildlife Sculpture
6553 Panton St.
Kilbride, Ontario L0P 1G0
CANADA
416-335-2512

Master Paint Systems
P.O. Box 1320
Loganville, GA 30249
800-334-8012

Montana Decoy Co.
Route 1
Box 251
Wilsall, MT 59086
406-578-2235

Northwest Carving Supply
P.O. Box 5211
216 West Ridge
Bozeman, MT 59715
406-587-8057

Denny Rogers
309 Daisy Ln.
Normal, IL 61761
309-452-8005

Ross Tool Co.
257 Queen Street, West
Toronto, Ontario M5V 1Z4
CANADA
416-598-2498

Sand-Rite Mfg. Co.
1611 N. Sheffield Ave.
Chicago, IL 60614
312-642-7287

Seto Co., Inc.
"Serabian Tool Co."
P.O. Box 148
195 Highway 36
West Keansburg, NJ 07734
201-495-0040

Tool Bin
10575 Clark Rd.
Davisburg, MI 48019
313-625-0390

Troy Woodcraft
301 Scottsdale Dr.
Troy, MI 48084
313-689-1997

Veasey Studios
955 Blue Ball Rd.
Elkton, MD 21921
301-392-3850

Joe Veracke and Assoc.
P.O. Box 48962
Chicago, IL 60648
312-824-9696

Valley Carving Studio
1720 Ellington Rd.
South Windsor, CT 06074

Warren Tool Co.
Rt. 1 14AS
Rhinebeck, NY 12572
914-876-7817

Welbeck Sawmill Ltd.
R. R. 2
Durham, Ontario N0G 1R0
CANADA
519-369-2144

Wildlife Carvings Supply
317 Holyoke Ave.
Beach Haven, NJ 08008
609-492-1871

Wildlife Woodcarvers
Avian Art, Inc.
4288 Staunton Dr.
Swartz Creek, MI 48473
313-732-6300

Wood Carvers Supply Co.
3056 Excelsior Blvd.
Minneapolis, MN 55416
612-927-7491

Wood Carvers Supply, Inc.
P.O. Box 8928
Norfolk, VA 23503
804-583-8928

Woodcraft Supply
41 Atlantic Ave.
Box 4000
Woburn, MA 01888
800-225-1153

Wood-Regan Instrument Co.
Vermiculation Pen
107 Forest St.
Montclair, NJ 07042

Books
Books Plus
133 St. Joseph's Blvd.
P.O. Box 731
Lodi, NJ 07644
201-777-3033

Highwood Bookshop
P.O. Box 1246
Traverse City, MI 49684
616-271-3898

Burning Tools
Chesterfield Craft Shop
P.O. Box 208
Chesterfield, NJ 08620

Colwood Electronics
715 Westwood Ave.
Long Branch, NJ 07740
201-222-2568

Hot Tools
7 Hawkes St.
P.O. Box 615
Marblehead, MA 01945
617-639-1000

The Detail Master
Leisure Time Products
2 Hillview Dr.
Barrington, IL 60010

Carving Knives
Cheston Knotts
106 S. Ford Ave.
Wilmington, DE 19805
302-652-5046

Lominack Knives
P.O. Box 1189
Abingdon, VA 24210
703-628-6591

Makepeace
1482 Maple Ave.
Paoli, PA 19301
215-644-6318

Fish Patterns
Bob Berry
2261 Runabout Place
El Cajon, CA 92019
619–588–7141

Fish Paint Schedules
Wildlife Artist Supply
  Company
360 Highway 78
P.O. Box 1330-B
Loganville, GA 30249
1-800-334-8012

Fish Reference Photos
Don Frank
7812 Westridge
Raytown, MO 64138
816-356-1990

Glass Eyes
Carvers Eye
P.O. Box 16692
Portland, OR 97216

Eyes
9630 Dundalk
Spring, TX 77379
713-376-2897

Hutch Decoy Carving Ltd.
7715 Warsaw Ave.
Glen Burnie, MD 21061
301-437-2501

Schoepfer Eyes
138 West 31st St.
New York, NY 10001
212-736-6934

Robert J. Smith
14900 W. 31st Ave.
Golden, CO 80401
303-278-1828

Tohickon Glass Eyes
P.O. Box 15
Erwinna, PA 18920
800-441-5983

Grinding Tool Burrs and
  Accessories
Pfingst & Company, Inc.
P.O. Box 377
South Plainfield, NJ 07080

Gamzon Bros. Inc.
21 W. 46th St.
New York, NY 10036
212-719-2550
800-223-6464

Paints and Brushes
Jim and Beebe Hopper
731 Beech Ave.
Chula Vista, CA 92010
619-420-8766

Christian J. Hummul Co.
404 Brooklets Ave.
Easton, MD 21601
301-636-2232

Windsor & Newton Inc.
555 Winsor Dr.
Secaucus, NJ 07094
201-864-9100

Ruby Carvers
Elkay Products Co.
1506 Sylvan Glade
Austin, TX 78745
512-441-1155

Wooden Bases
Birds of a Feather
Box 386
41 Edstrom Rd.
Marlborough, CT 06447
203-295-9469

Ken Thomas Bases
1909 Woodstream Dr.
York, PA 17402

Display Cases
Rioux's Wildlife in Wood
   and Pewter
P.O. Box 3008
Syracuse, NY 13220-3008

Commercial Fish Blanks

Fish can be copied on duplicating lathes.
Blanks are identical in shape to the original master model carved by the artist.
They can be sanded smooth and painted, or finely detailed, then finished with any kind of base work desired. Big Sky Carvers in Bozeman, Montana carries several different fish blanks, and will be carrying a series of Bob Berry freshwater fish blanks in the near future.

Contact:
   Big Sky Carvers
   8256 Huffine Lane
   Bozeman, MT 59715